Junya Ishigami

Published under license from Editorial Gustavo Gili. *2G* was founded in 1997 as an international architecture magazine by Editorial Gustavo Gili, evolving, over the years, into a monographic magazine and international reference. Since 2016 it is published under license by Koenig Books.

Director and editor Moisés Puente

Graphic design RafamateoStudio

Translation Emma Cypher-Dournes & Beth Gelb, Paul Hammond

Proofreading Paul Hammond

Cover photograph Satoru Emoto

Lithography Rovira Digital, Barcelona

Print agpograf impressors, Barcelona

First published by Koenig Books

Koenig Books Ltd
At the Serpentine Gallery
Kensington Gardens
London W2 3XA
www.koenigbooks.co.uk

Printed in Spain
ISBN: 978-3-96098-096-4

Distribution

Germany, Austria and Switzerland
Buchhandlung Walther König, Cologne
Tel. +49 (0) 221 / 20 59 6-53
Fax +49 (0) 221 / 20 59 6-60
verlag@buchhandlung-walther-koenig.de

Distribution outside the United States and Canada, Germany, Austria and Switzerland
Thames & Hudson Ltd., London
www.thamesandhudson.com

United States and Canada
D.A.P. / Distributed Art Publishers, Inc., New York
www.artbook.com

MIX
Paper | Supporting responsible forestry
FSC® C104592

Architecture and sympathy

I think that to some extent architecture needs to be compatible with any place and any time. In modern architecture, and other previous styles, there was always a form of architecture that was sought after in that particular period of time. Nevertheless, it is necessary to think about a condition of architecture that embodies more diverse values and that can respond to various kinds of environments. In order to do this, rather than coming up with a single answer from within this variety of values and ways of thinking, it is important to think about the various ways that architecture can exist. Otherwise, contemporary architecture as we know it would no longer be compatible with the times.

The modern era placed the greatest emphasis on function, which served as a fundamental condition

Kayoko Ota is an architectural curator based in Tokyo and a founding partner of PLAT, a platform for enhancing architectural thinking in socially engaged cultural and educational projects. After ten years at AMO, the creative think-tank arm of OMA in Rotterdam, she returned to Tokyo to curate the Japanese Pavilion at the 2014 Venice Biennale of Architecture. This conversation was hold in February 2018.

Contents

for building architecture. For this reason building types were designed to fit their intended functions. We would no longer be able to create what the world asks of us if we did not propose a form of architecture that fits with the conditions of each individual human being, environment, and place, rather than something that is attributed to a particular framework. To think about an architecture that can respond to this sense of diversity, I began to feel it necessary to consider architecture in a freer way. I really think it is important that we do this.

About exhibitions

When working on exhibitions I try not to distinguish or create a clear division between installation and architecture. Even within the context of architecture there are numerous projects that the architect can engage with, such as designing the interiors of buildings, proposals for urban planning, housing complexes, private residences, and commercial facilities. Architects create spaces on various sites and under various conditions, and until now I had considered it plausible to create installations by looking at the museum as one such site. In that sense works like Balloon and Table were built as specific forms of architecture and could only have been realized in that particular site.

Balloon, Contemporary Art Museum, Tokyo, Japan, 2007-2008.

Table, 2015-2010.

There is also this sense of me wanting to take a step backwards to gain a commanding view and to think about my actual ideas and thought processes. I try and organize and bring everything together over a long period of time. As in any project, it is not possible to contemplate architectural works through a commanding perspective. Working in a museum space, however, enables me to engage with architecture in this way, and there are indeed things that I can only do when presented with this kind of opportunity. Rather than using the museum as a site on which to create new architecture—like an installation, for instance, which would be another project in its own right—I would like to use it as a means to step back and revisit my works, as I rarely have the chance to do this.

I really think it's important to try and develop this idea of seeking a new way of thinking about architecture. This is something I attempted to do for the exhibition *Freeing Architecture* at the Fondation Cartier in Paris in 2018, where I tried to show and communicate my own way of thinking about architecture by introducing specific examples of the architectural works I am currently working on.

Disclosing the concept

I am particularly conscious of how a strong concept, form or presence can be powerfully effective and appealing, yet can in certain contexts rebuff or repel people who feel no strong attraction to it. Architecture needs to communicate its potential abilities to many people, and for that purpose should convey the most important part of its concept. It is not possible to do this if people are unable to access the architecture due to being overwhelmed by the concept before entering. More and more people would refrain from engaging with architecture if its concept were obvious from the outset.

Those who dislike red, for example, would most probably stay away from a red building or one built around that color concept. When thinking about the purpose for which you want to use red as a means of expression, as opposed to simply a desire to appropriate it, there is no need to disclose the color from the beginning. Should the red remain unseen, then those who dislike red would enter the building and engage with it. This is something I consider very important. Take a revolution for instance. Rather than bringing about a certain change that presents a clear before and after in terms of revolution, it is important to enable something to permeate circumstances without our knowledge. This permeability exerts greater power and influence. In order to create and increase this sense of permeability, rather than creating a strong, hard shell around the concept it is important to disclose its very nature. For this reason, I begin by first coming up with a strong concept within my mind from which to develop my ideas, but from there on in I engage in a long process of gently and clearly unraveling it.

KAIT Workshop

In KAIT Workshop there are many columns distributed throughout the space. The concept itself is centered on there being many columns, yet were these columns to feel overwhelming or cumbersome the space would simply end there. In other words, the concept is weakened in terms of its persuasive power and people would no longer want to be there in the first place. To avoid this kind of outcome I considered ways of how I could realize my concept of having many columns without necessarily making it feel that way. As the client was a university and many teachers were involved it was necessary to listen to all sorts of requests. However, each teacher only spoke in relation to their own department or field of expertise, as in a teacher from the automobile department talking only about cars, and so on. The space, of course, is not solely used by that particular person, hence it should not be just a space about cars (nor a space about computers alone, say). As such, at a certain point I realized it would not work to have a layout in which the columns were simply arranged in accordance with a grid. I thought about how I could create a space that reflected these various demands yet at the same time be interpreted in different ways to some extent. I eventually arrived at the idea of arranging the columns randomly to create an uneven space, rather than an even and homogenous one.

Naturalness

All architectural aspects and qualities that have persisted until now have probably been able to do so because they seem natural. Be it a column or a beam, one presumes that its most comprehensively natural form was selected via the creating of numerous structures on our earth, as well as homes for people to live in. This naturalness is what is important, I feel, like the naturalness that resides in things created by the human hand. It's very important to me to be able to feel something is natural or to sense a certain atmosphere that is only attainable through a natural thing. No matter how new something may be, it would not work if it did not appear natural. This "naturalness" can be a powerful force in architecture.

The essence of architecture

One client asked me to create a building with a longstanding feel to it. Usually such places have come down to us from the past and have become what they are over the course of time, and thus there are not many cases of embarking on one from scratch. There is this notion that something becomes better with age, and unless this kind of atmosphere is established from the first it would be like dining on the first floor of a brand new office building—which, of course, would be pretty bland and tasteless. In other words, what was asked of me was to create something that didn't look as if it had just been built. What the client was talking about here was the essence of architecture, in that things that have become better as a result of changes through time have a completely different meaning to something created as a decoration, such as a theme park. The issue involves considering what one must do in order to build something that has a connection to the essence of architecture. The project itself was to devise an architectural plan which would somehow result in such an outcome.

The individual and composition

In terms of fashion, it would be rather embarrassing to wear clothes that have been designed according to one's individuality alone. You really couldn't walk down the street wearing something like that, or at least that's what I think. Your own individuality is in fact not just built upon your set of values but is what exists within the personal sense of balance you find while taking these various values into consideration.

In the context of architecture, when building a house you need to take into account the surrounding environment; the neighboring houses, for instance. You cannot simply create something that reflects your own personal values. In that respect, when trying to find your own place in the world, rather than creating a concept in a hard, shell-like manner I believe it's particularly important to establish a condition in which the concept becomes something that disseminates itself naturally.

It is somewhat ordinary to have unique values and perhaps there is no harm in conveying them. That said, because each and every one of us is simultaneously involved in constructing the world it is tacitly understood that we must try to find a sense of balance. I think it's more difficult to focus one's energy on these things.

To some extent we can accept that everyone creates unique things, which are individual to that person. I believe it's more difficult for us to create something we can all share, something which becomes pivotal to today's architecture.

Considering something as preexisting

What I probably think about is how I'd feel towards something if I considered it to have been preexisting in that place. Let's say I envision a certain building. I think to myself how I would feel if that building were to have already existed there for ten years, for example. So, rather than the process in which something is realized and arrives at completion, what, to put it simply, is realistically more important to me is the process by which the architecture I build deteriorates or is destroyed. I think that even a hundred years after its construction a building needs to maintain a certain quality of space. For instance, I was deeply moved when I visited the Parthenon. No matter how decayed and aged the structure may be, you can still sense its strength as a space. At the same time I don't think it would have been such a magnificent building were it not built in that location on a rocky mountain. I probably would not have been as moved if the building had been located in the middle of the city. In other words I think it's quite rare for a building to attain a degree of sympathy on its own. The strength of a particular building increases by its taking into account the surrounding environment as a whole, including the landscape and the people who live there.

Something that has subsisted over a long period of time harbors an overwhelming amount of information, as well as other accumulated aspects. This is something I can by no means create, which is why I am so strongly attracted to it.

Architecture

When told you can create any kind of "architecture" as freely as you wish, in the end it comes down to the issue of what in fact constitutes something as being architecture. When you build a work there needs to be a certain quality that everyone finds essentially architectural, which I would call a sense of "architectural-ness." Without such a quality the work would no longer be free and could even end up not existing. I believe architecture as a medium will always remain and will continue to be sought after by people in times to come. It is important to note that what causes a piece of architecture to be architectural is that it is free.

The architect

Going back to what I mentioned at the outset, the role of an architect is similar to a tour guide who comfortably leads you into a new world. As an architect I want to create architecture that leads people to various places with comfort and ease, no matter how hard it may be to go there. I'm always thinking about how I can succeed in optimally achieving this, and guiding people in the best way possible.

KAIT Workshop, Kanagawa

2004-2008

This building of workshops for the students of Kanagawa Institute of Technology (KAIT) is located next to the campus central square. With its slightly rhomboid 2,000 m^2 footprint, four glazed façades and longitudinal roof lanterns, the building has 305 pillars, rectangular in section and of different sizes but all extremely slender, which seem to be randomly placed although they are perfectly calculated to look like a kind of constellation or forest. In turn, along with the roof beams, the building has an excellent anti-seismic performance. The density of the pillars varies in different areas, as does their disposition in relation to the axes, meaning that the overall vision is at odds with the order of a grid, in which users can interpret the space of a system that does not divulge any control on the part of the architect. The different density, orientation and section of the pillars means that the view of the building's supports changes as one moves through the building, extending from their quasi-disappearance to areas that are more shielded. Between these pillars wood and ceramic workshops, engineering machinery and offices are organized in a concept of abstract "flexibility" capable of accommodating different functions without the need for compartmentalization, providing users with fluid circulation through the building and different ways of appropriating their workspaces.

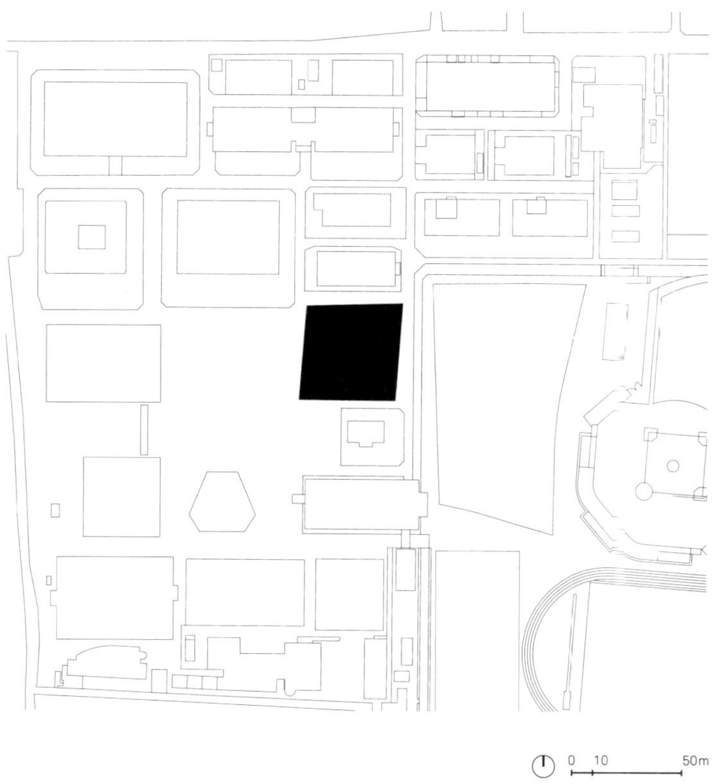

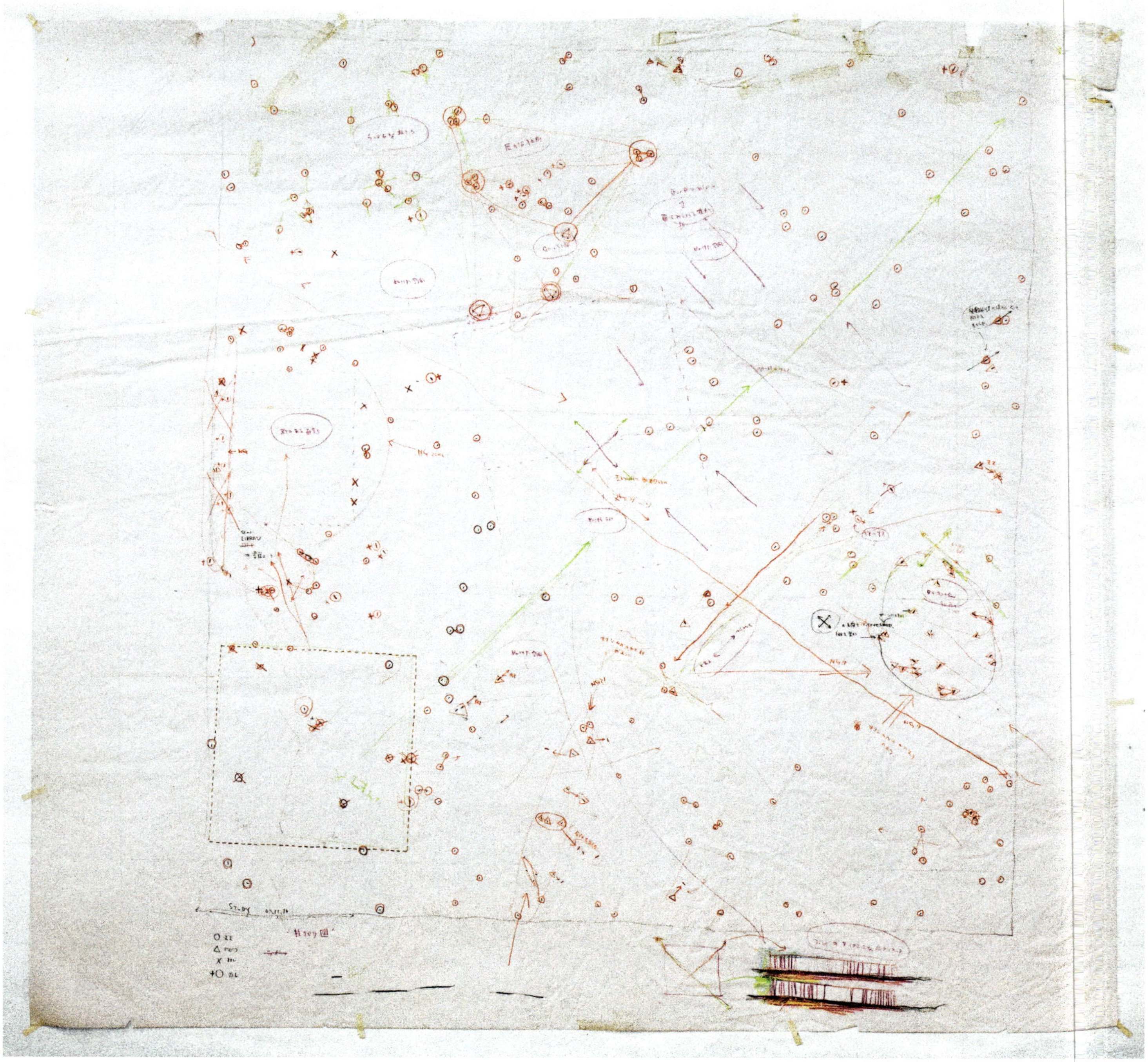

Original sketches

KAIT Workshop, Kanagawa

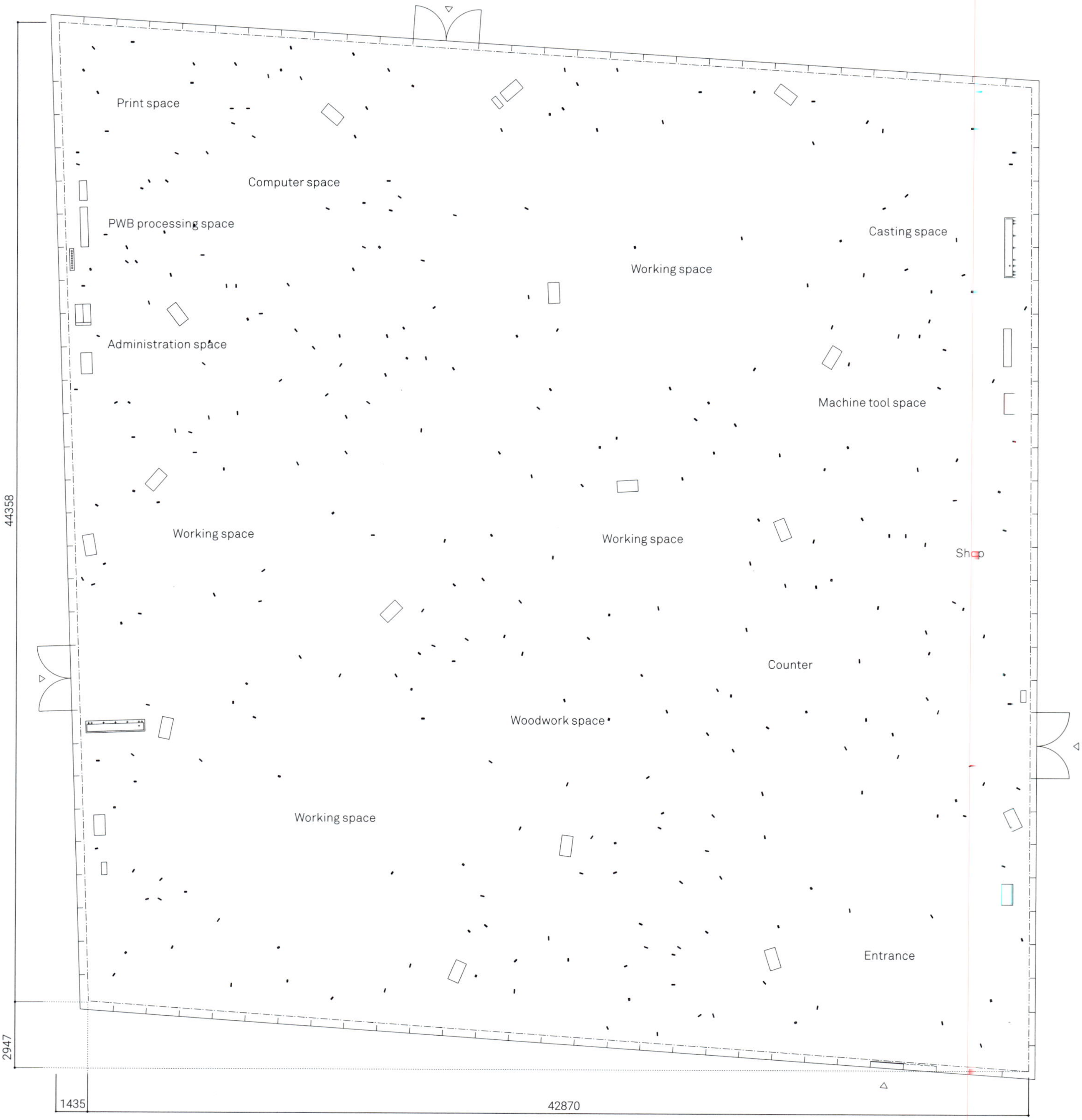
Print space
Computer space
PWB processing space
Administration space
Working space
Casting space
Machine tool space
Working space
Working space
Shop
Counter
Woodwork space
Working space
Entrance
44358
2947
1435
42870

Floor plan

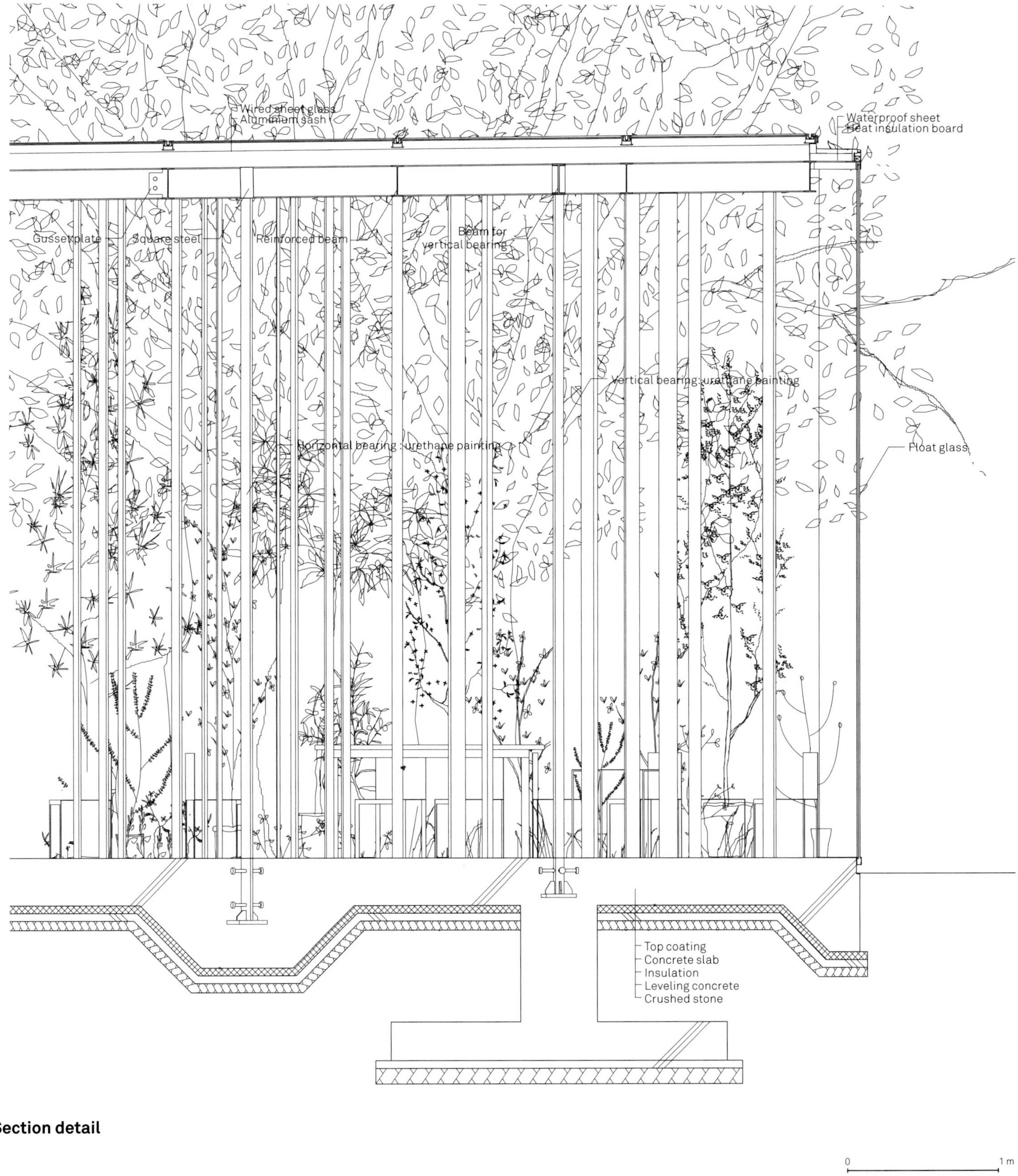

Section detail

Column Number
Width
Thickness
Angle
Height
Column Type
Material
T
W
A

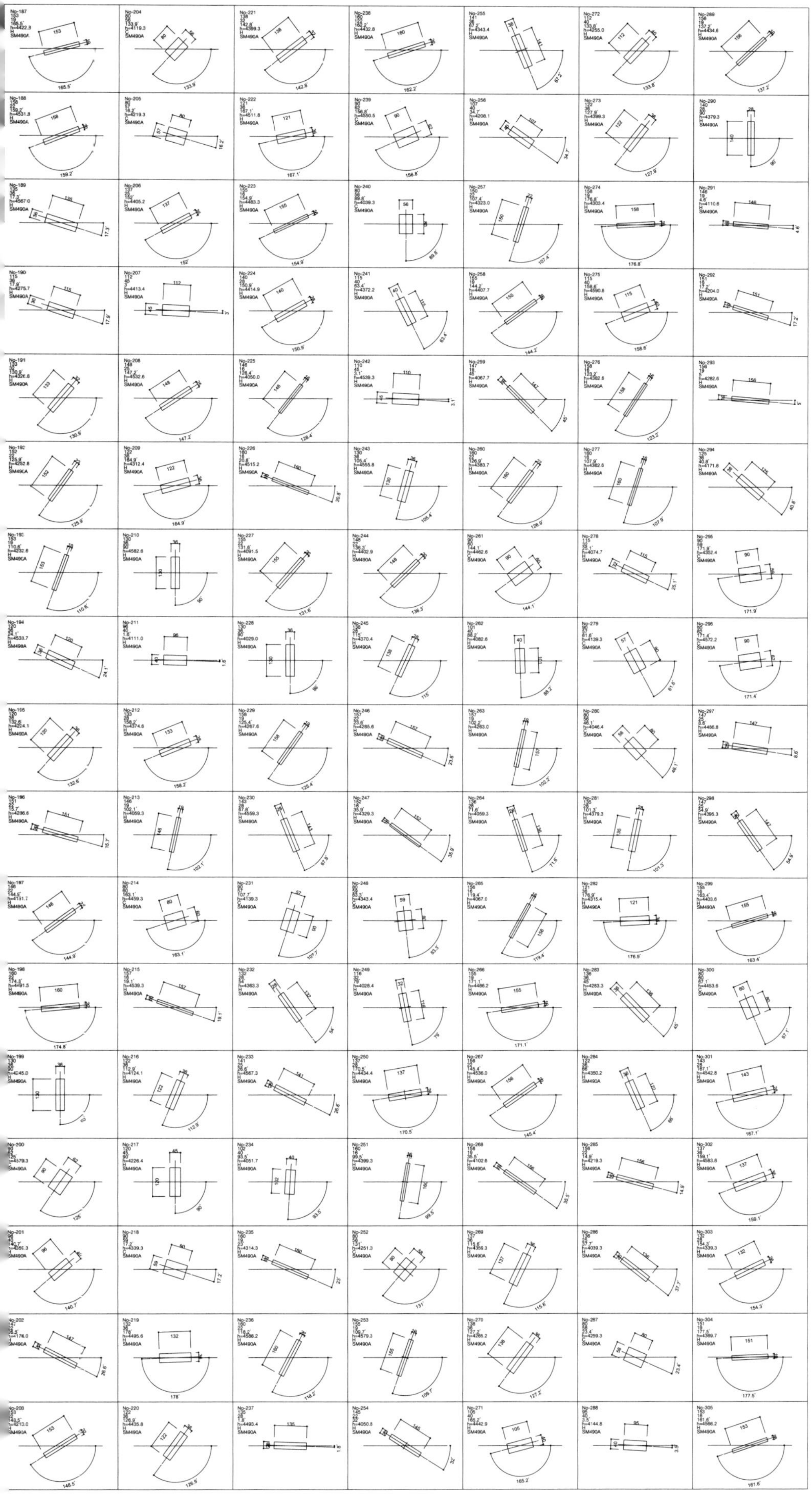

List of the 305 pillars

Yohji Yamamoto Store, New York

2006-2008

This project involves the remodeling of an industrial building to house Yohji Yamamoto's flagship store between Gansevoort Street and 13 West Street in New York's Meatpacking District. The old triangular brick building from the 1960s is of some 1,500 m^2, but the proprietor only had the 250 m^2 of the prow-shaped point available. The principal operation involves cutting into the building and opening up a private street that divided the building in two parts, shaped like a piece of pie, one intended for the shop per se, and the other for the warehouse. Access to the shop is effected from this private street, which the sales assistants use in their comings and goings between warehouse and store. Another of the project decisions was to alter the old snub-nosed corner and make it sharp-pointed, thereby accentuating its prow-like quality within the dense urban weave.

The bricks from the demolition were reused for the new façade, like some kind of a Lego set, and the window spaces of the store were regularized and sealed with frameless glass, such that the city enters into the store and traverses it. The interior is very simple, not at all overdesigned, and avails itself of a new system of hangers and the furnishings required for the shop. The project intervenes at both the scale of the city and as an architectural project that extends to the interior design.

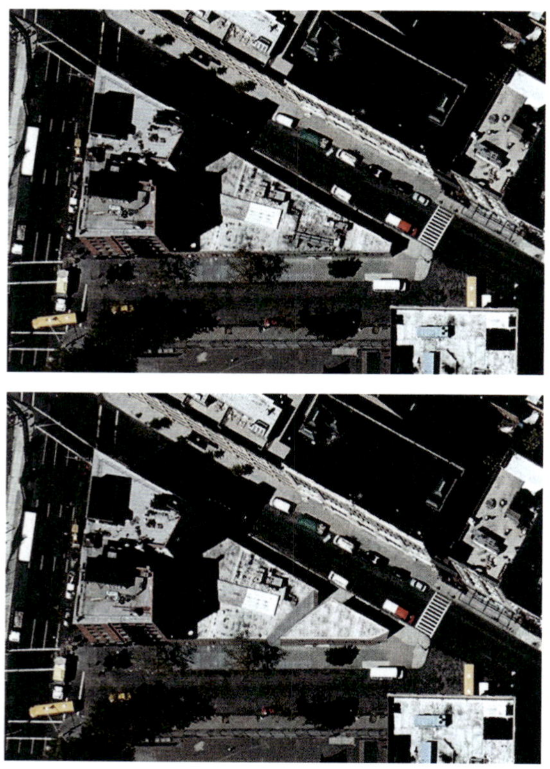

Before and after

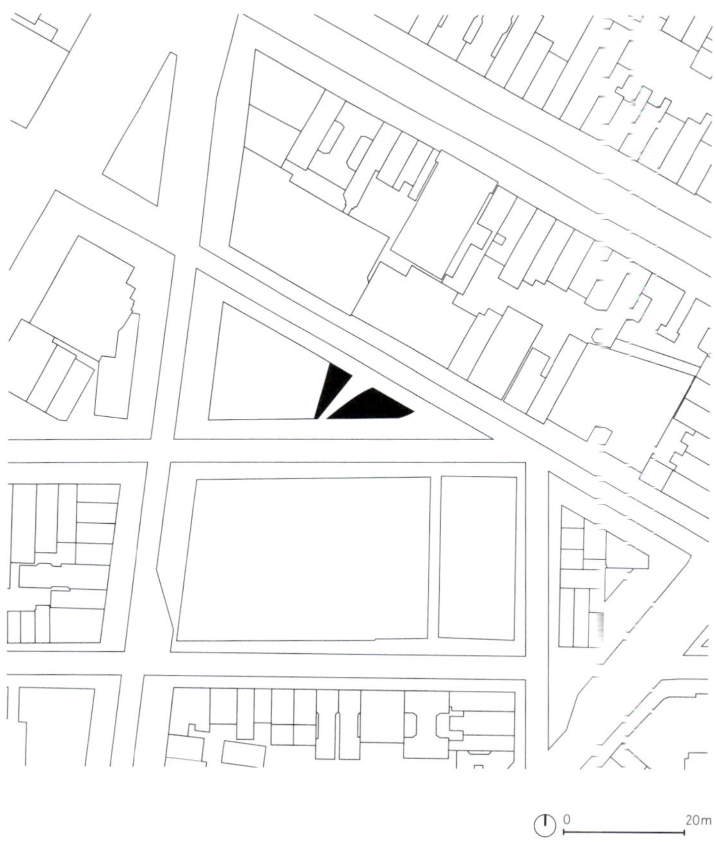

XING
SCHOOL

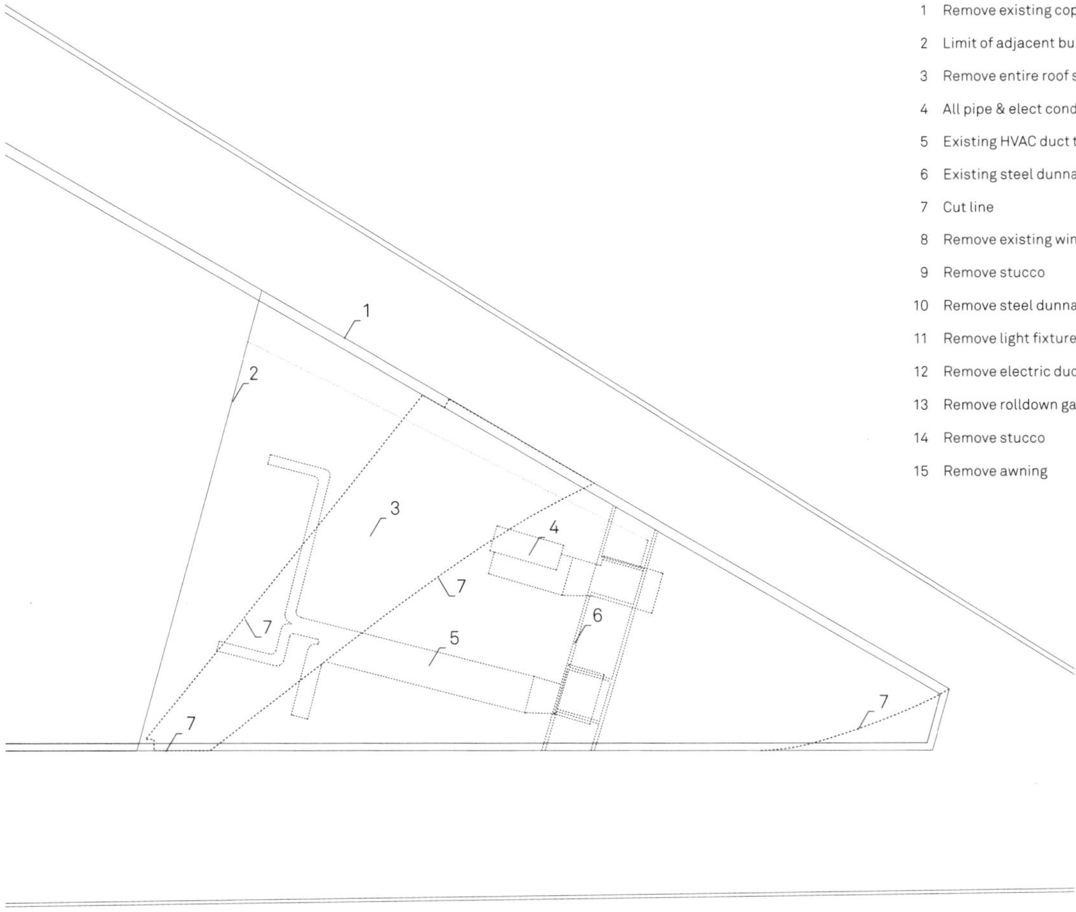

1 Remove existing copings
2 Limit of adjacent building
3 Remove entire roof structure
4 All pipe & elect conduits to be removed
5 Existing HVAC duct to be removed
6 Existing steel dunnage to be removed
7 Cut line
8 Remove existing windows
9 Remove stucco
10 Remove steel dunnage
11 Remove light fixtures
12 Remove electric duct
13 Remove rolldown gate
14 Remove stucco
15 Remove awning

Existing roof plan

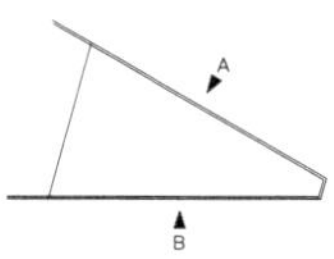

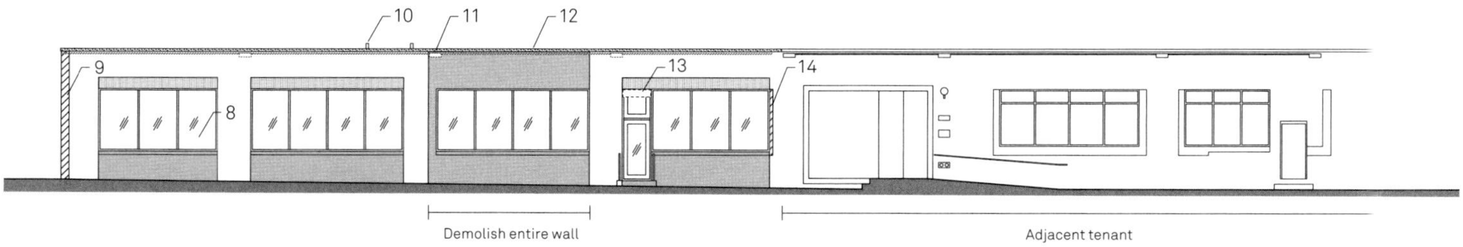

A

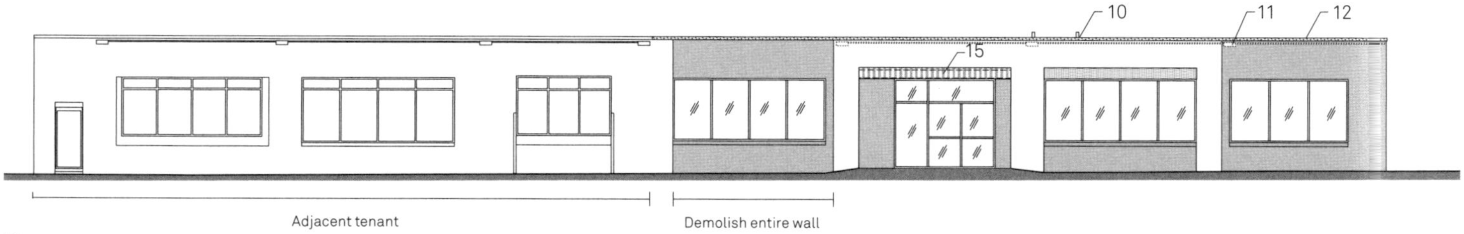

B

Existing elevation

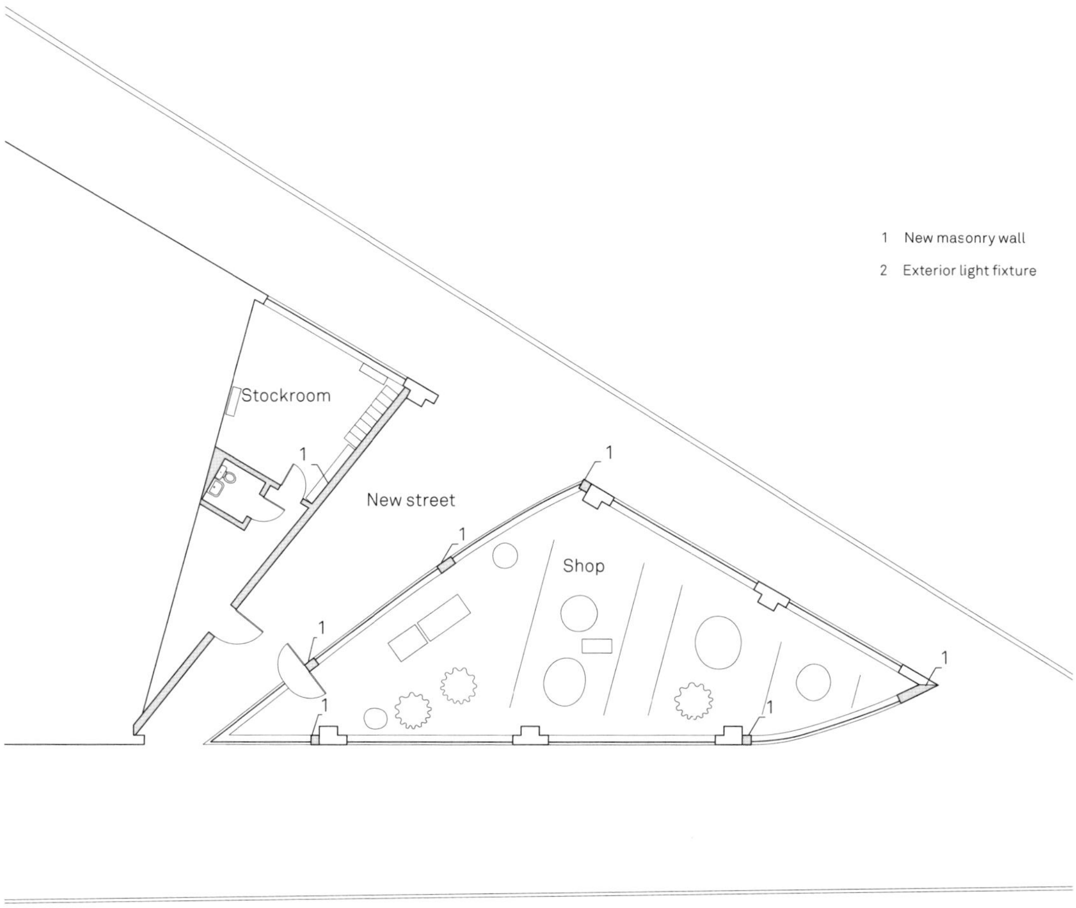

1 New masonry wall

2 Exterior light fixture

New floor plan

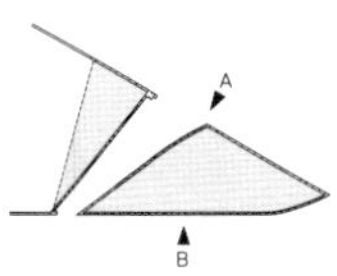

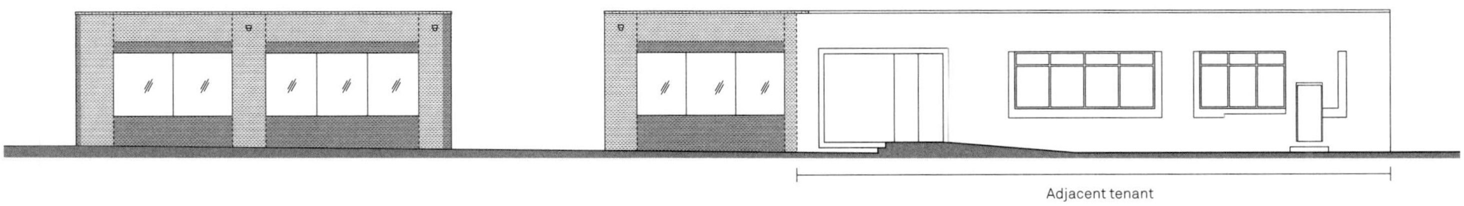

A

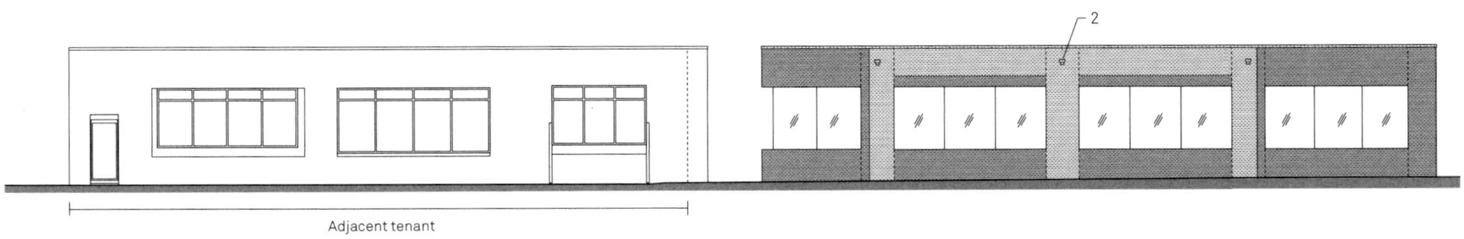

B

New elevation

Yohji Yamamoto Store, New York

EXIT

Japanese Pavillon, 11th International Architecture Biennale, Venice

2008

Junya Ishigami took charge of Japan's representation at the Venice Biennale's 11th International Architectural Exhibition in an intervention consisting of two parts. Firstly, he covered the walls of Japan's permanent pavilion, built by Takamasa Yoshizaka in 1956, with delicate hand-drawn images; and secondly, he built a series of greenhouses in the garden of the pavilion's own land lot.The proportions and sizes of the four greenhouses are in accordance with the trees and flowers in the existing environment; the way they grow, their forms and their required light conditions. The greenhouses are architecture and at the same time a new garden created within the pavilion's garden. They are not equipped with air-conditioning facilities. They are not designed to create extreme environments for a collection of plants from different parts of the world, as in a typical botanical garden that houses tropical plants in cold locations.

Of course, the intervention is essentially concerned with gathering plants that would never naturally grow in Venice; however the project merely creates a minute environmental change that gives a slight fluctuation to the existing environment (climate). As a result the architecture itself becomes equivalent to the plants. A new environment is created on this site through intermixing the existing landscape, the new plants, and the four greenhouses. As the light conditions are constantly changing, at times the glass reflects the peripheral scenery while on a different side it appears transparent. These ever-changing sceneries are blended one with the other, creating a beautiful landscape that wavers marvelously on the site.

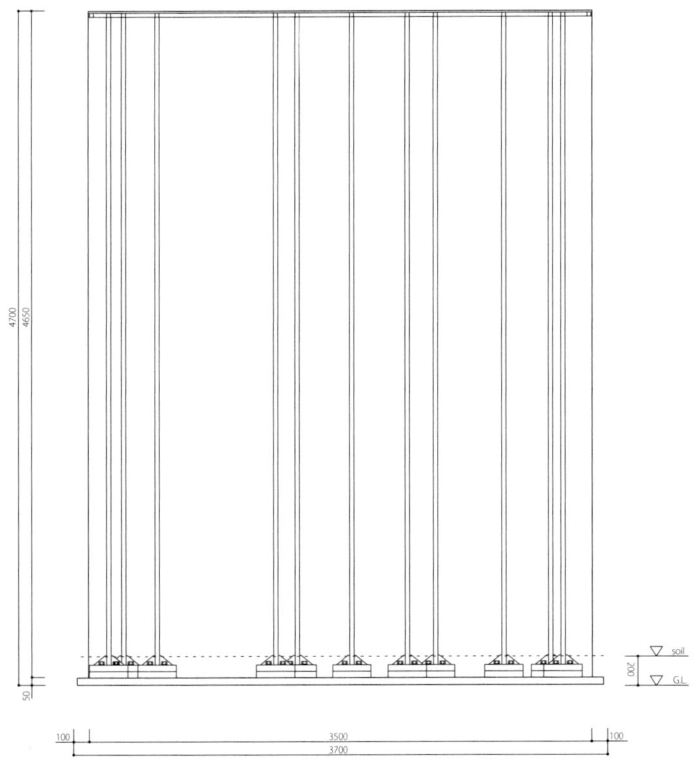

1

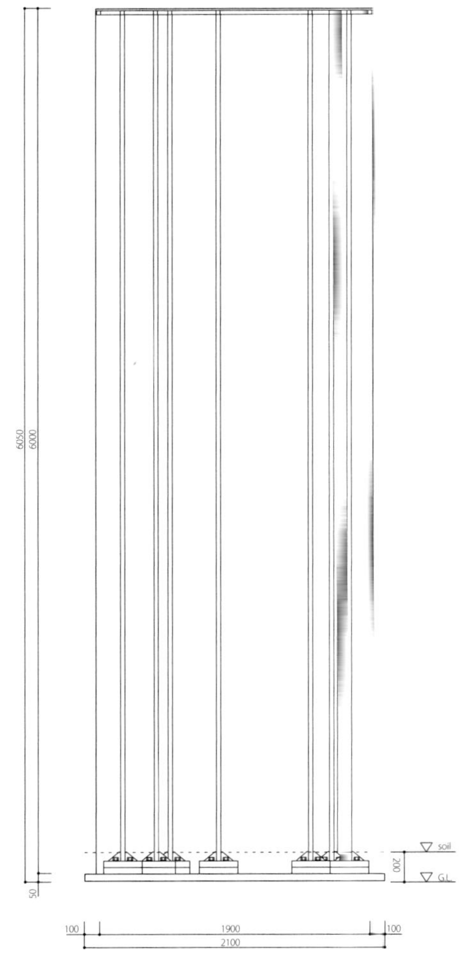

2

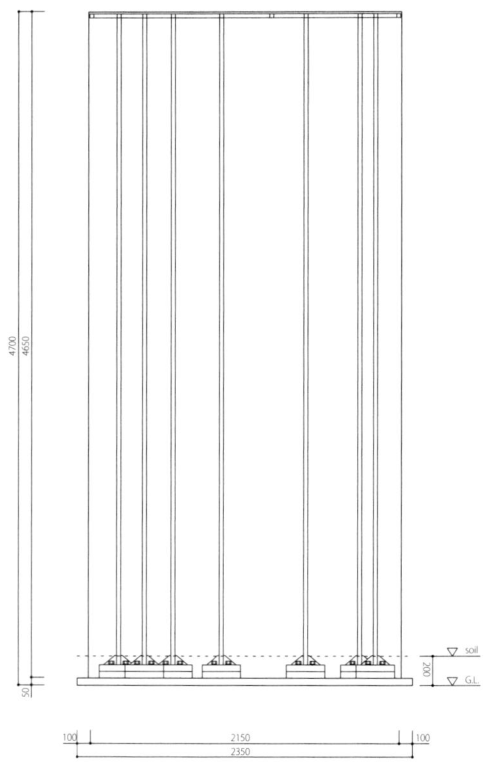

3

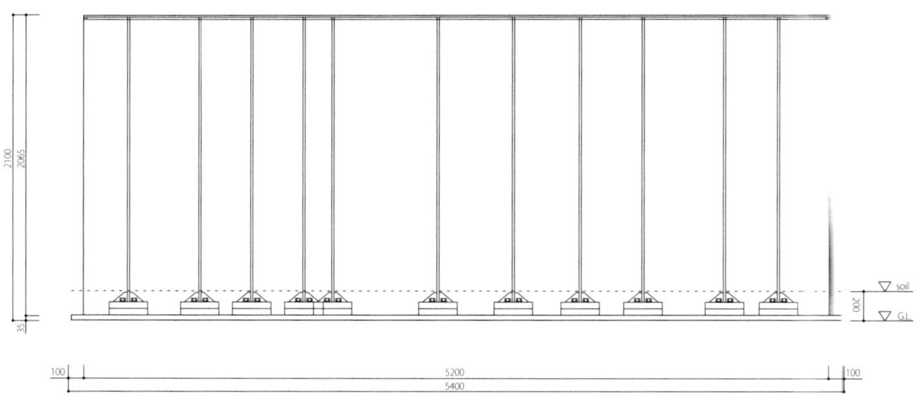

4

Little garden pavilions. Sections

Elevation

Floor plan

Multipurpose Plaza, Kanagawa

2008-

This multipurpose semi-covered plaza is situated on the campus of the Kanagawa Institute of Technology (KAIT), very close to KAIT Workshop, and is intended for different student activities, ranging from events, barbecues and parties to the practice of sports or as a relaxation area, and also as a shady area in the hot summer months.

It is a single-story building some 100 m long and 60 m wide, with a height clearance that averages 2.3 m with no pillars as intermediary support. The space consists of a roof made of a single steel sheet, 12 mm thick, supported by four lateral perimeter walls and punctuated with multiple overhead apertures open to the sky. In fine weather, soft light filters in through the skylights; when it rains, droplets fall freely through the openings so that a lot of rain pillars appear in the space.

The water from the rooftop flows along the surface and falls through a single opening, creating a small waterfall inside the building. As a result, the heigh of the space inside changes according to the weather. It is similar to the phenomenon of weather changing the heigh of the clouds, that changes the heigh of the sky. Covered with mortar and gravel, the bowl-shaped floor traces the same shape as the slight caternary curvature of the roof. The vast interior is a very wide and flat space, formed by the curved roof and the curved floor. With a floor like the earth and a ceiling like the sky, the two seem to merge to form a horizon in the distance, giving an impression of infinite space.

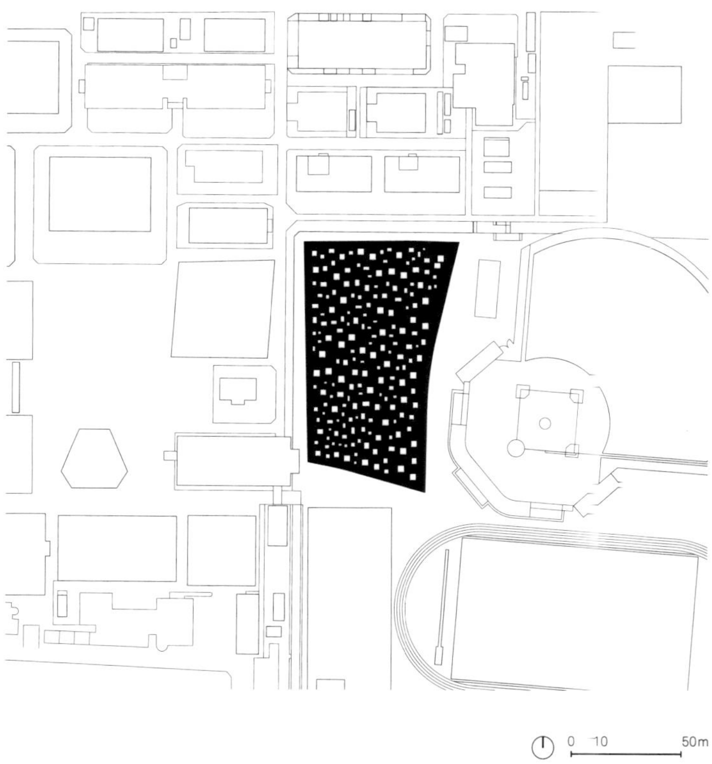

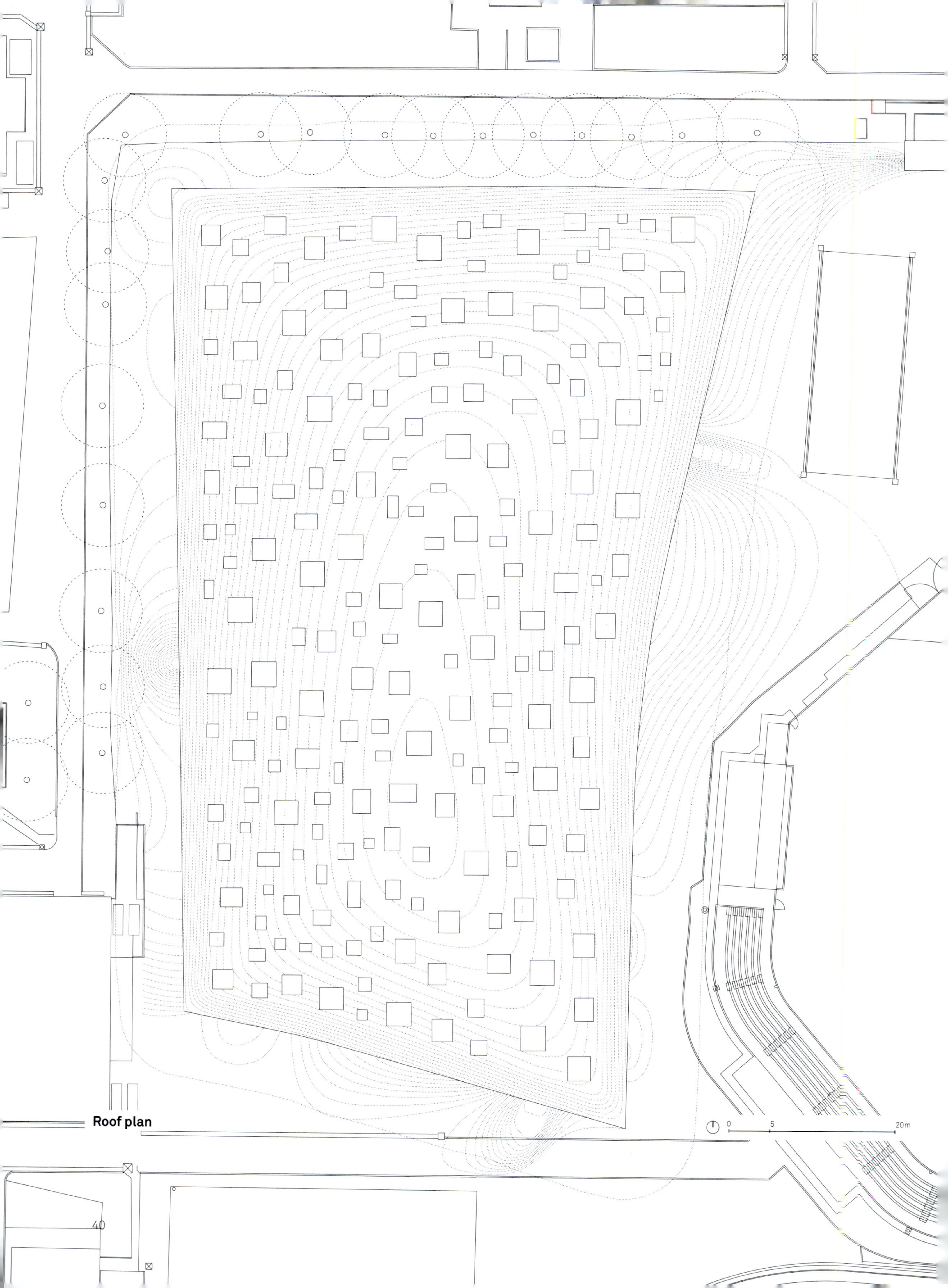

Roof plan

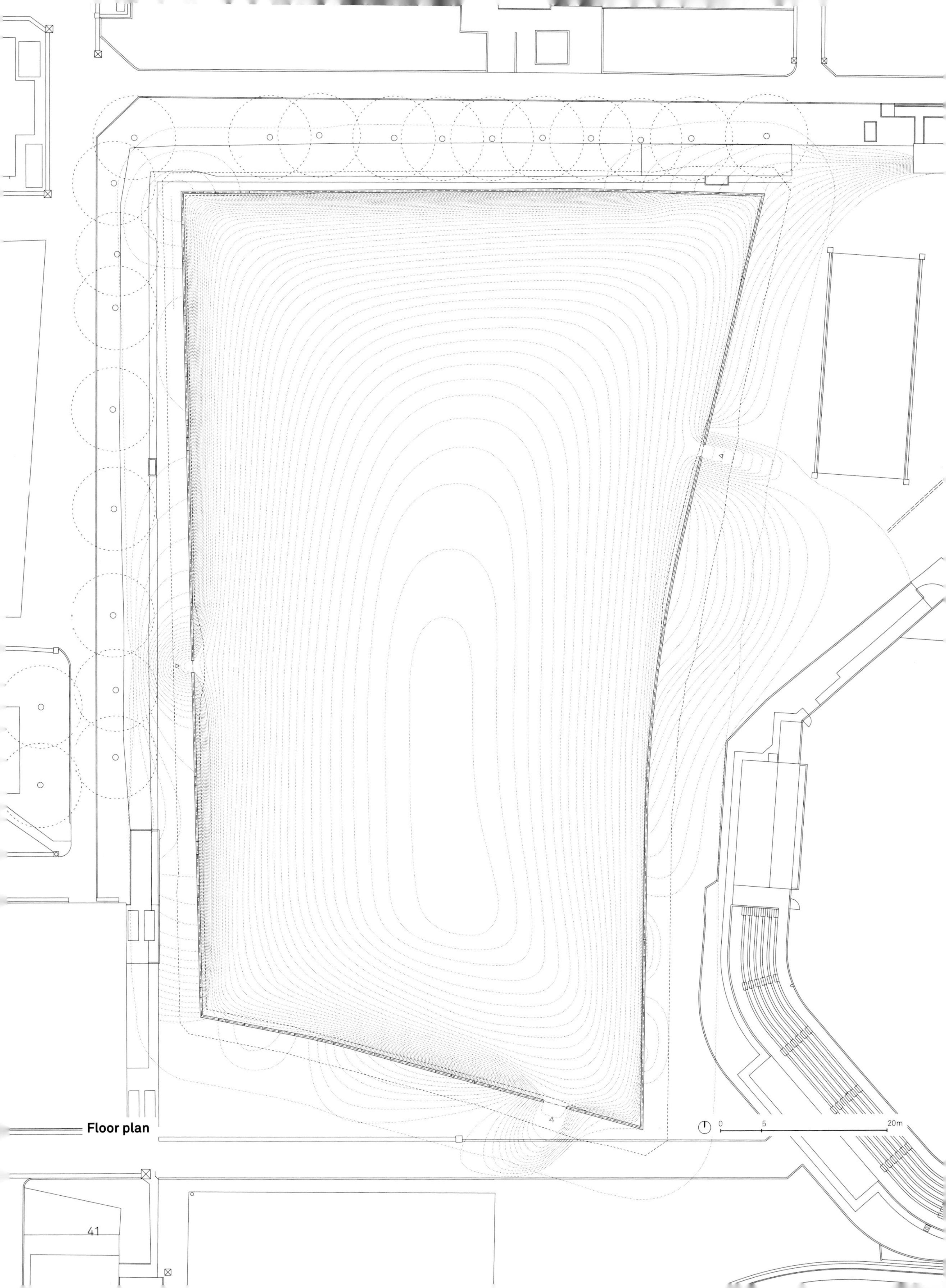

Floor plan

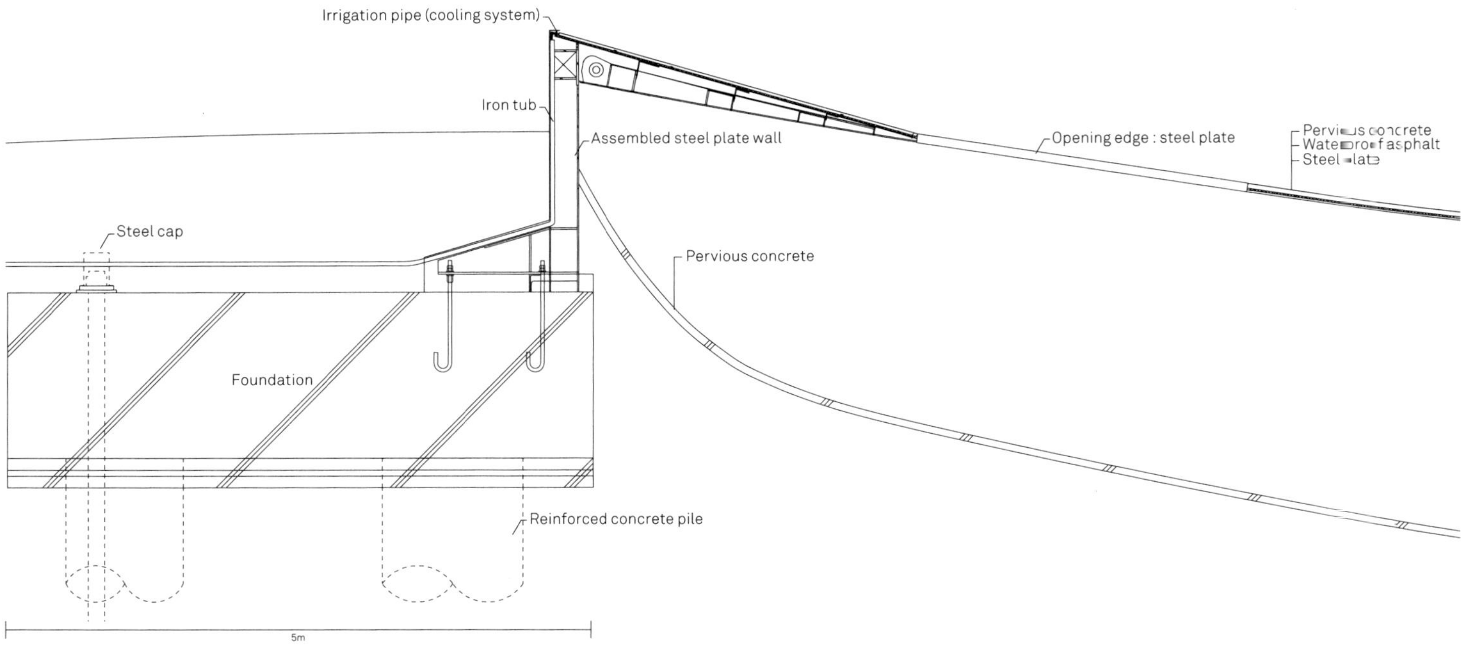

Section detail

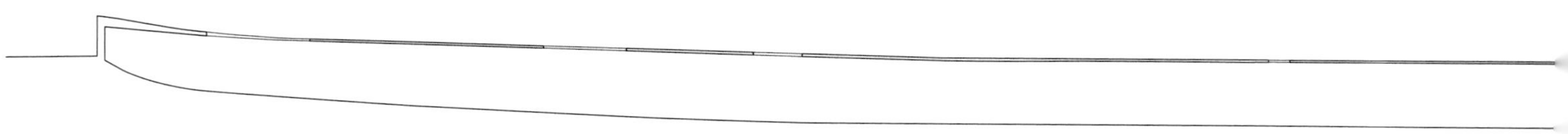

Section

Mockup

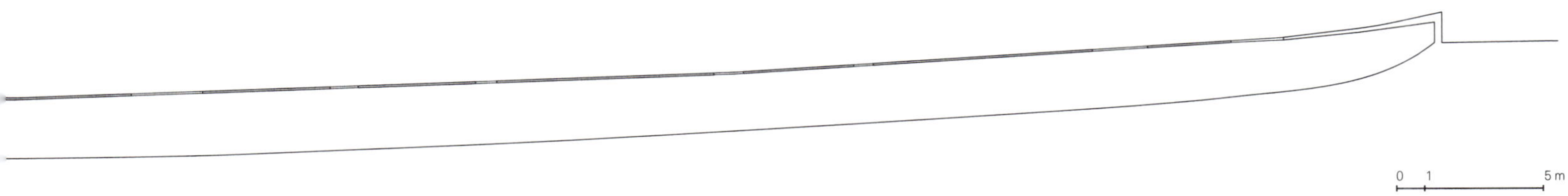

House with plants

2010-2012

This house for a young couple is situated in an urban area on the outskirts of Tokyo. The clients spend much of their time in the urban environments of their workplaces, so that the house sets out to provide them with a more natural refuge in which time slows down, enabling the rhythms of nature and of the changing seasons to be contemplated in a more leisurely way. Accordingly, despite being a first residence the house is conceived as a holiday villa in which to enjoy the time spent in it to the full, to feel at home in, and to seek refuge from the hostile urban environment.

The house has a very simple cubic form, with 15 mm wide non-structural outer walls positioned on a very fine metal framework. These panels constitute the exterior walls of a building punctuated with large openings.

The natural terrain is conserved in part of the inside of the house, in which various kinds of plants grow. On the ground floor different spaces are arranged, with the simple furnishings, the vegetation and the architecture forming the elements of an interior domestic landscape. The earthen floor is reminiscent of the traditional Japanese house's *doma*—an earthen pit devoted to the cooking and conservation of food—and the *niwa*—a term that evokes an idea of a "garden" in the contemporary context—with the garden here inverting the binary opposition of interior/exterior. Another living space, situated on a mezzanine level and accessible via a ladder, seems to float above the plants.

Concept drawings

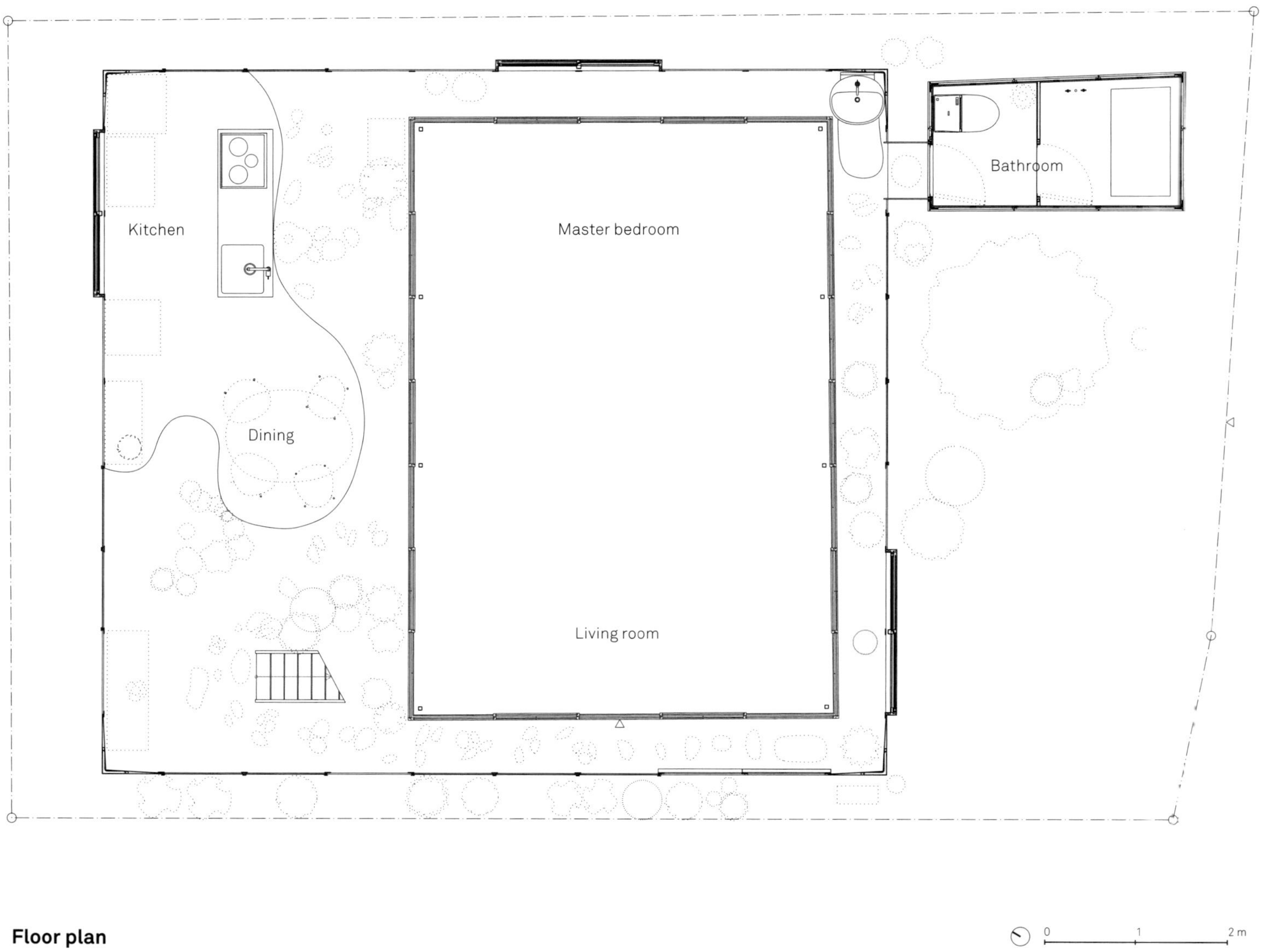

Floor plan

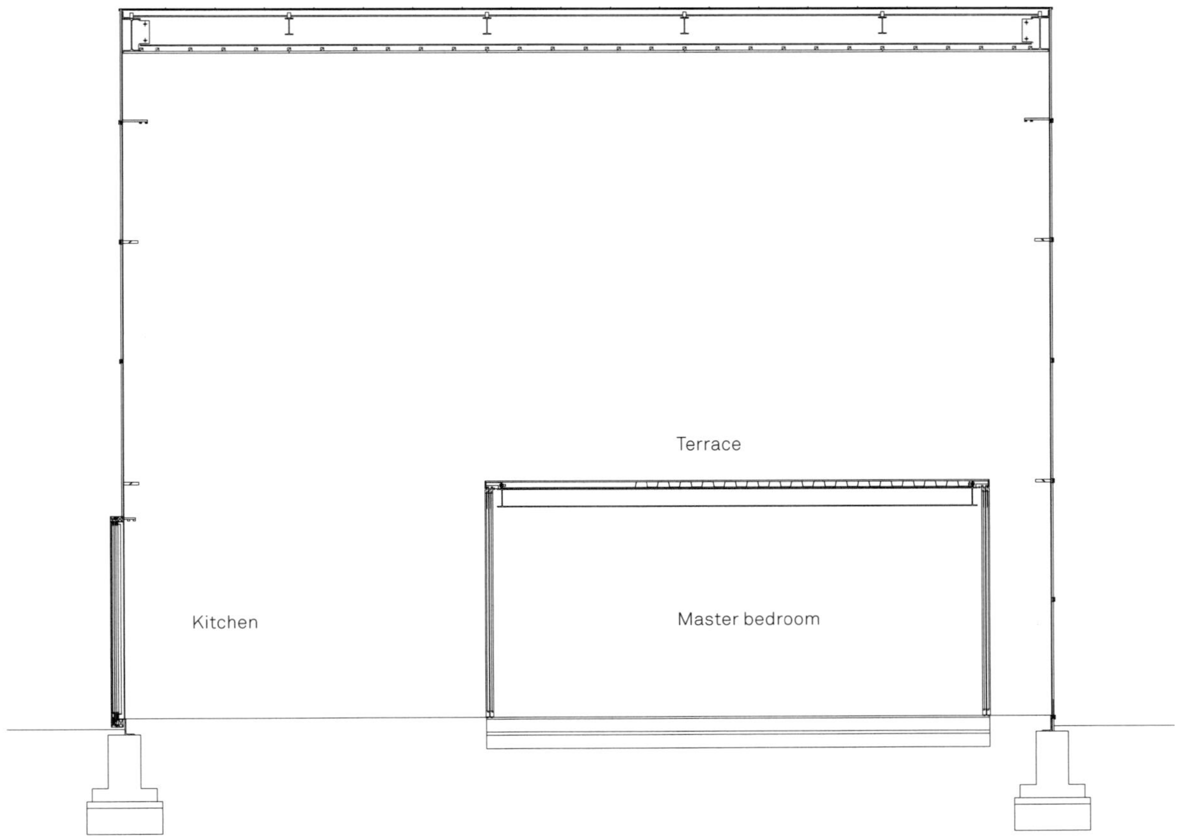

Section

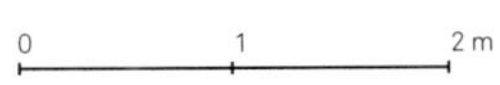

Polytechnic Museum, Moscow

2012-

The new Polytechnic Museum in Moscow occupies an existing building from the turn of the nineteenth century which occupies an entire city block and has a surface area of some 40,000 m^2. A detailed survey showed the building to be in very good condition above ground, yet with significant deterioration underground and in the structure. As a result, the museum was restored above ground to its original state with minimal modification, while transforming the underground at a much larger scale to make a new ground floor for entry into the museum. In the basement, the labyrinth of existing brick walls was removed to leave only the pillars, which were reinforced as the sole elements to support the entire building. In doing so, a huge entrance space consisting of a myriad of columns emerges. The site was carved in a bowl shape to make a gently sloped landscape around the museum and connect the existing ground level with the basement level.

The existing elevation is raised by annexing the underground level, thereby achieving an entirely new proportion for the elevation. Without any addition to the existing museum, and through simply revealing what was formerly submerged below ground, the historical building is born anew.

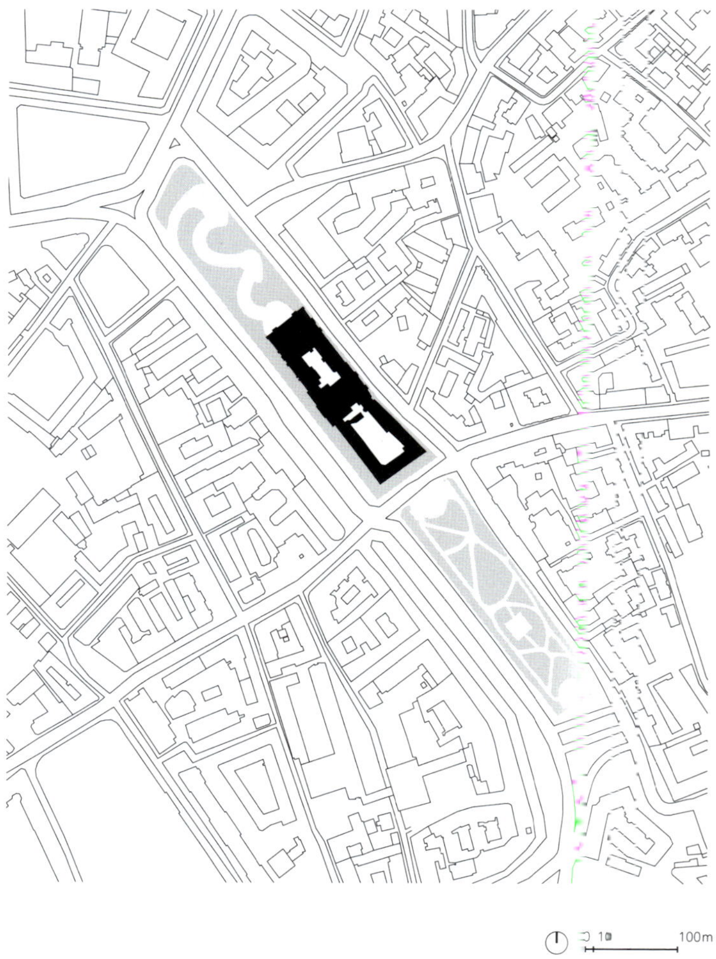

ПОД'ЕЗД №9

АРЕНДА
933·50·50

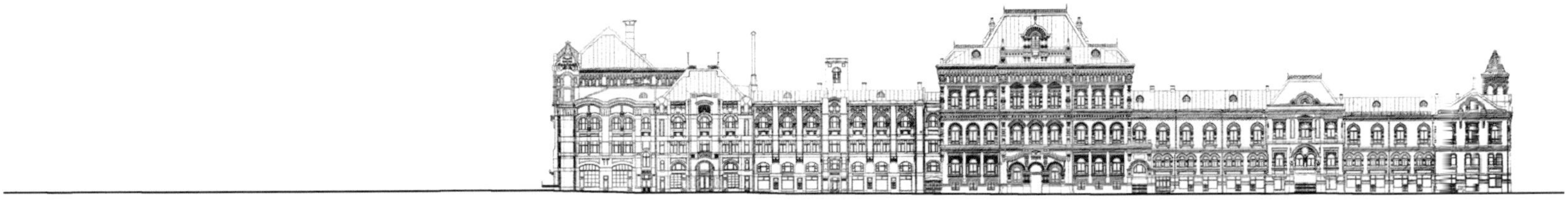

Existing elevation

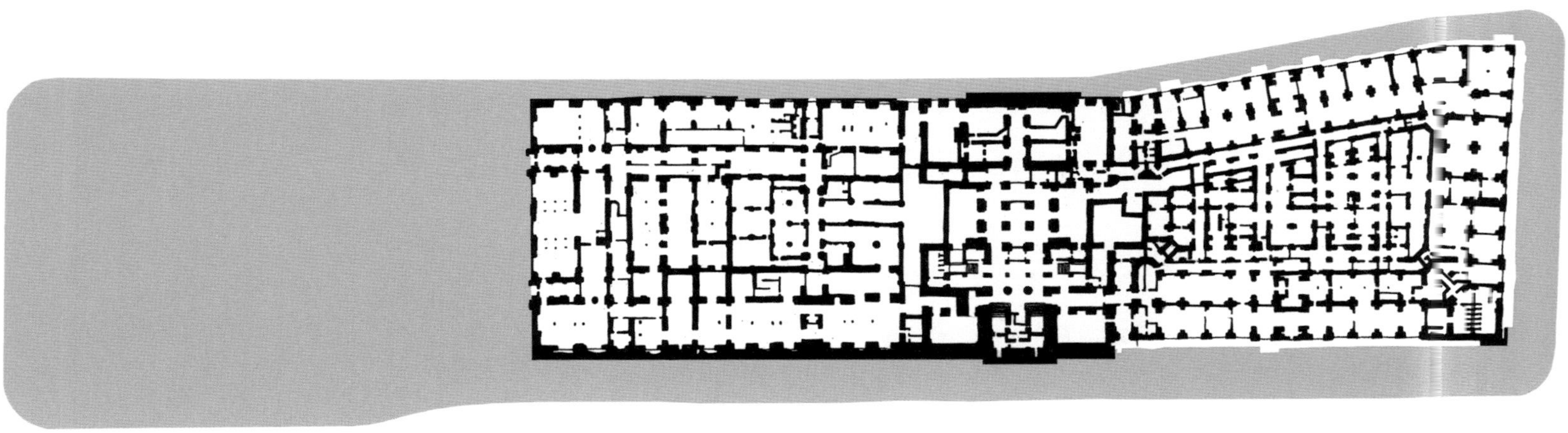

Existing basement floor plan

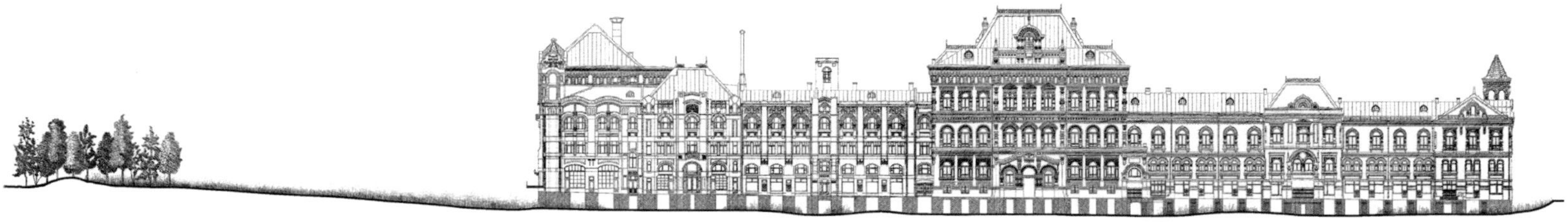

New elevation

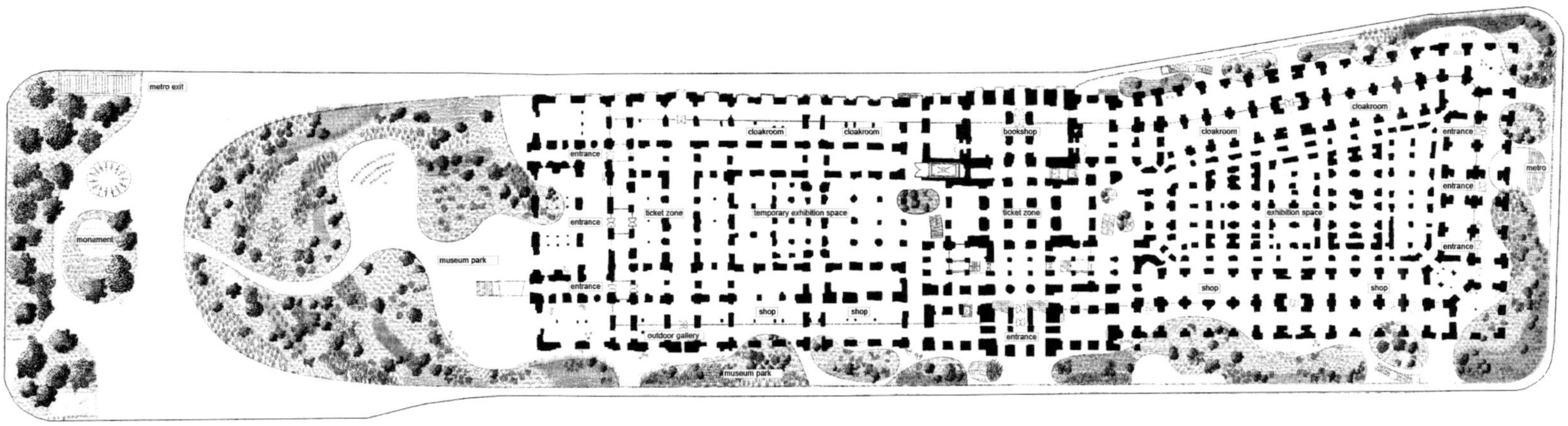

New basement floor plan

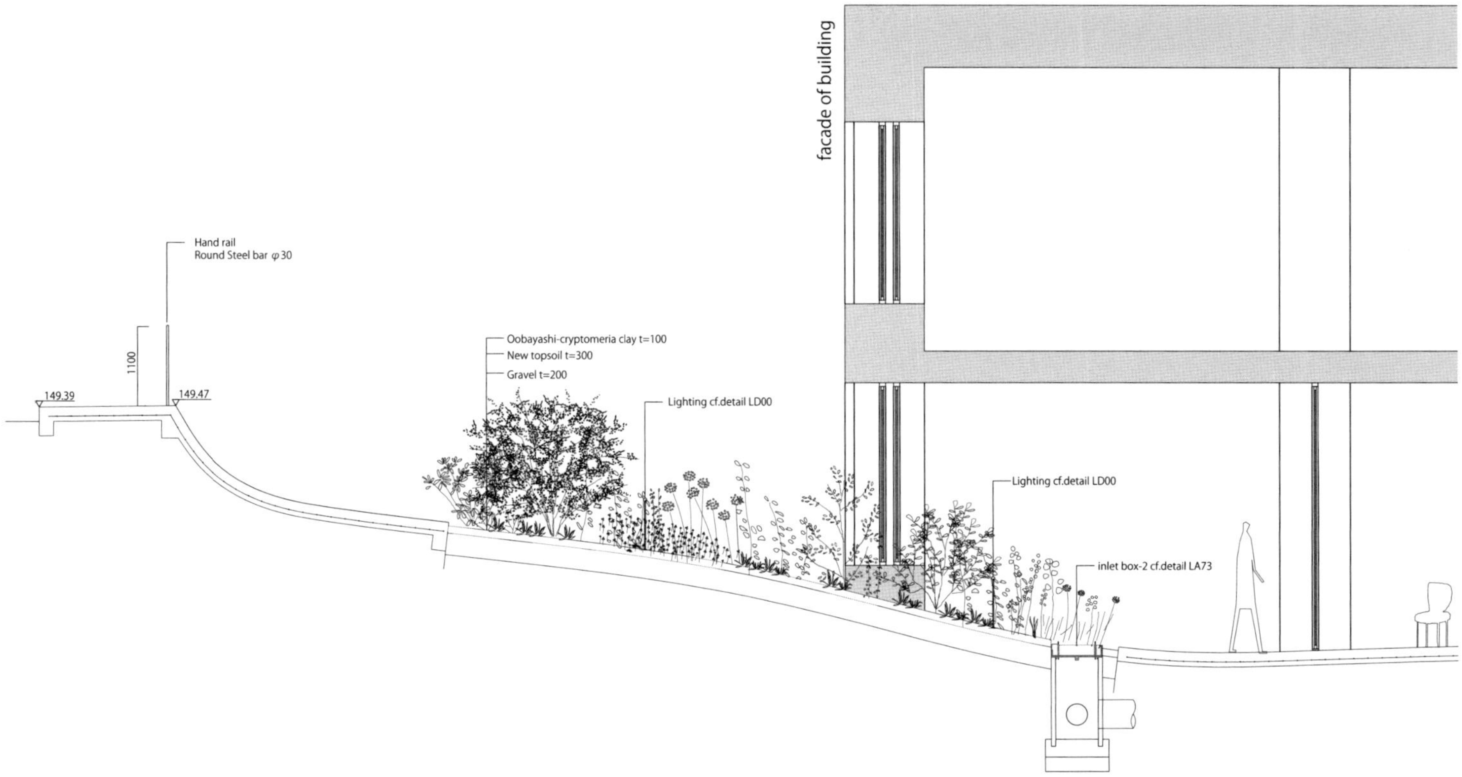

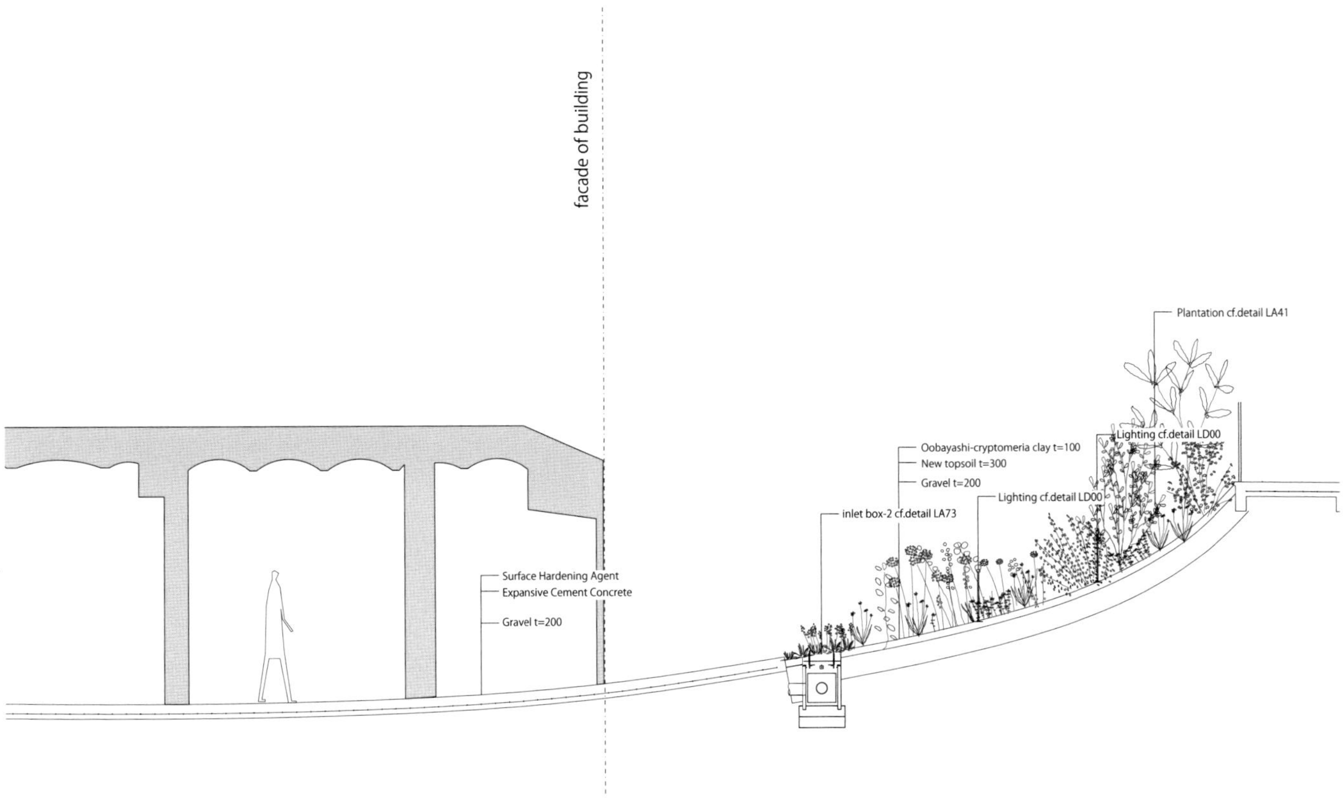

Sections detail

Park Groot Vijversburg Visitor Center, Tytsjerk

2012-2017

The site for Park Groot Vijversburg Visitor Center is a the garden of a wealthy summer house dating from the nineteenth century, situated in the north of The Netherlands, near Leeuwarden. Because the park was historically preserved and protected, any proposal could not change the existing environment at all, making it difficult to find an appropriate site for the new extension and the renovation of the existing villa. The project aims to preserve elements of the existing environment such as greenery, tree position, pond shape, etc., and simply traces the existing walking path to create the building's footprint. A glass screen is placed along the edge of the path to form the structure without pillars. The building is half buried in the ground, appearing to merge with the landscape. Made up of three winding corridors that come together to form a vast space destined to welcome visitors, this building rests entirely on structural glass walls, whose curves ensure the building's stability.

The entrance to one of the corridors adjoins a villa that is located in the center of the park, thereby constituting a contemporary extension of sorts to this historical house. The gently sloping corridor leads the visitor to the lecture hall area, offering unparalleled views of the surrounding landscape. The three glass corridors follow the already existing pathways, forming a transparent hedge, before progressively disappearing, making way for the park's avenues and pathways.

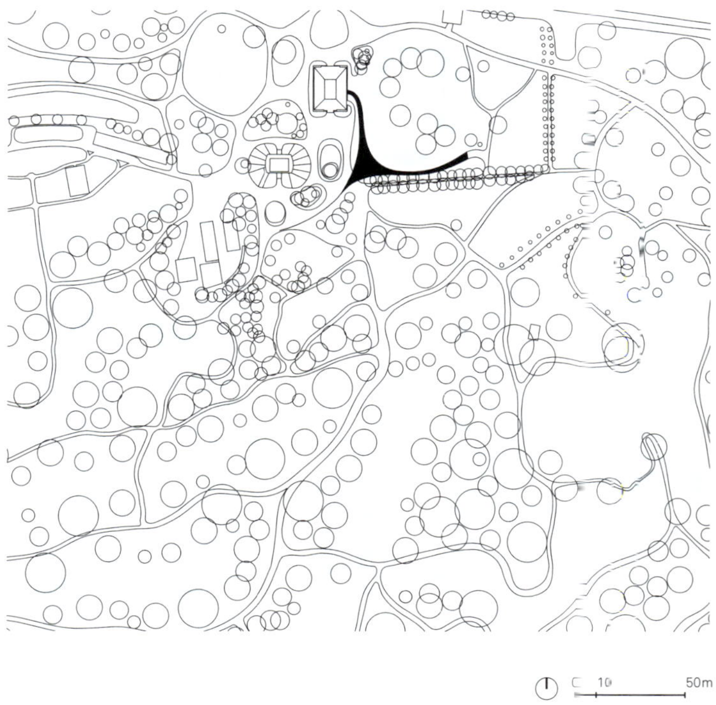

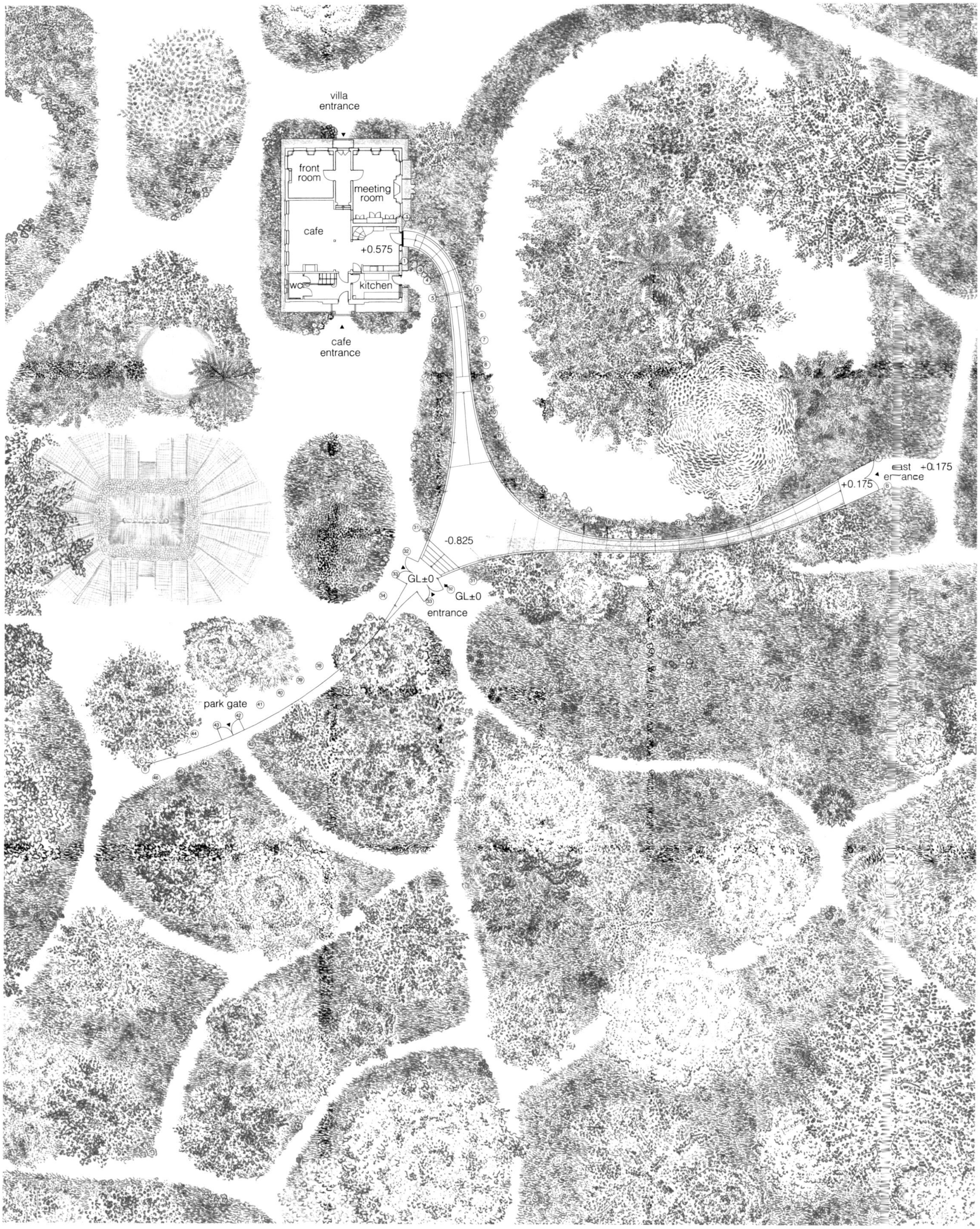
villa entrance
front room
meeting room
cafe
+0.575
wc
kitchen
cafe entrance
east entrance
+0.175
+0.175
-0.825
GL±0
GL±0
entrance
park gate
0 1 10 m

Floor plan

Elevations

0 1
10 m

Home for the elderly, Akita

2012-

This residence for elderly people suffering from senile dementia is located in Akita in northern Japan. In order to create a more familiar environment for the aged, the residence consists of a collection of traditional houses that will form a new ensemble with differentiated spaces. The idea was to salvage forty traditional houses from all over the country, houses which were due for demolition, by utilizing the age-old technique of *hikiya* (the transferring of a house from one place to another without dismantling its structure) which, through the use of trucks with a low chassis, would move them to their new location. Not all the features of the houses have been retained. Instead an attempt was made to abstract the particular characteristics of each of them, in order, through their combination, to create a new architecture in a new kind of village, in which some houses are converted into bedrooms alone, others into a dining room or a gallery.

Similarly, the gardens are constructed using stones and trees collected in different places, so that a certain sense of familiarity is restored to the residents due to them going back to living in spaces similar to those they've lived in as youngsters.

The carpentry, geographical origin, techniques, and local construction materials used give each of these houses its own unique identity. All of the living spaces have the same proportions, determined by the size of *tatami* mats. By assembling these unique houses, based on traditional proportions, a harmonious ensemble is created in which the residents can feel at home in the familiar setting of a traditional Japanese living space, and easily find their bearings.

Selected houses

Floor plans of selected houses

Kept parts of the houses

Private room
GL-725
F-2
WC
Office
Courtyard
Private room
GL-900
F-2
Private room
GL-900
F-2
Courtyard
Bath room
GL-935
F-2
Curtains
Dressing space
WC
Restroom
GL-830
F-2
Storage
GL±0
F-1
Courtyard
-670
Courtyard
-490
Courtyard
Dining room
GL-615
F-2
Kitchen
GL-775
F-2
Courtyard
Courtyard
Private room
GL-790
F-2
Private room
GL-790
F-2
-680
-615
Courtyard
-680
-510
Entrance
GL-610
F-1
Courtyard
Private room
GL-710
F-2
Courtyard
Private room
GL-650
F-2
Private room
GL-650
F-2
-710
-795
Private room
GL-795
F-2
WC
GL-805
F-2
-610
Gallery
GL-510
F-1
Courtyard
Frontyard
Parts liable to catch fire: 3m
3000

Floor plan

Private room
GL-1005
F-2
Courtyard
Private room
GL-555
F-2
WC
GL-455
F-2
Bath room
GL-610
F-2
Curtains
Dressing space
WC
Private room
GL-940
F-2
Courtyard
Restroom
GL-455
F-2
Courtyard
Private room
GL-625
F-2
Public space
GL-280
F-2
Courtyard
-390
Courtyard
Dining room
GL-355
F-2
Courtyard
Office
GL-725
F-2
Courtyard
Courtyard
Courtyard
Kitchen
GL-405
F-2
Courtyard
Private room
GL-660
F-2
Entrance
GL-610
F-1
-660
Private room
GL-660
F-2
Restroom
GL-610
F-2
Courtyard
Courtyard
Restroom
GL-610
F-2
WC
Private room
GL-610
F-2
Private room
GL-680
F-2
Private room
GL-705
F-2
Courtyard

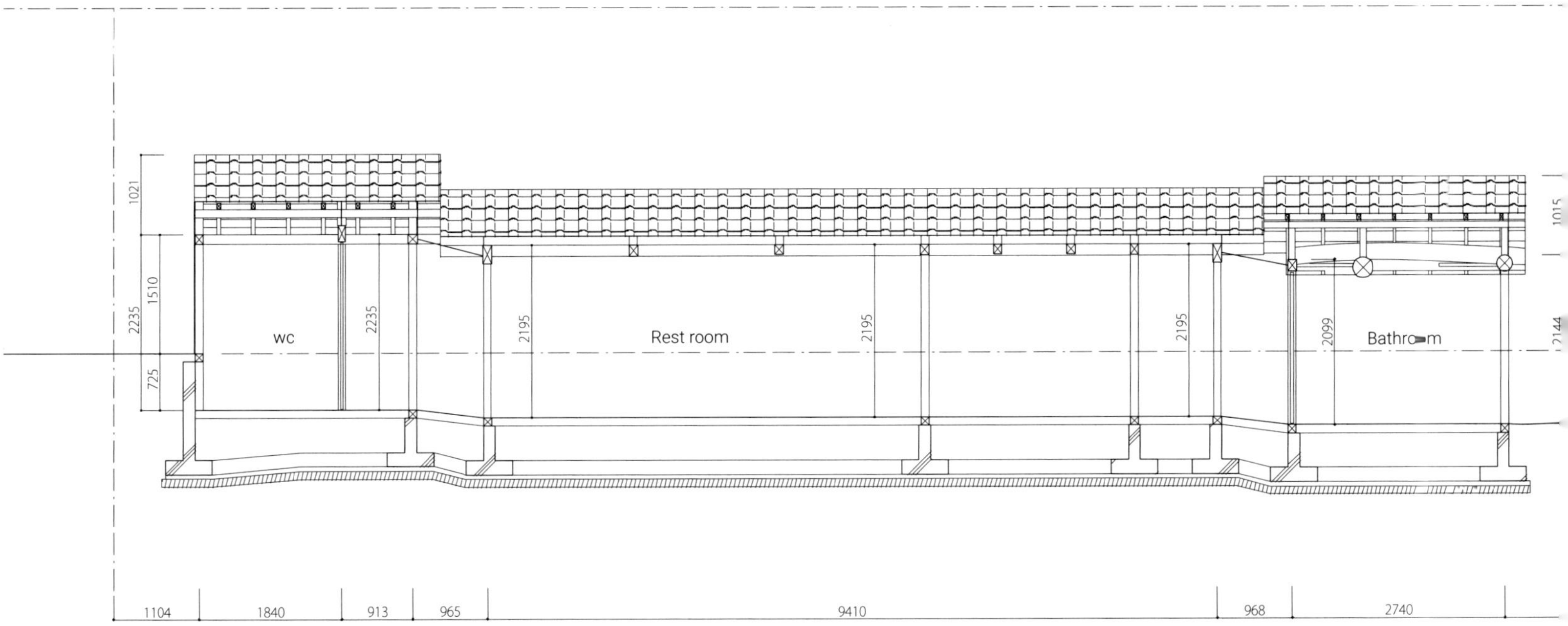
1021
1510
2235
725
WC
2235
2195
Rest room
2195
2195
2099
Bathroom
1015
2144
1104
1840
913
965
9410
968
2740

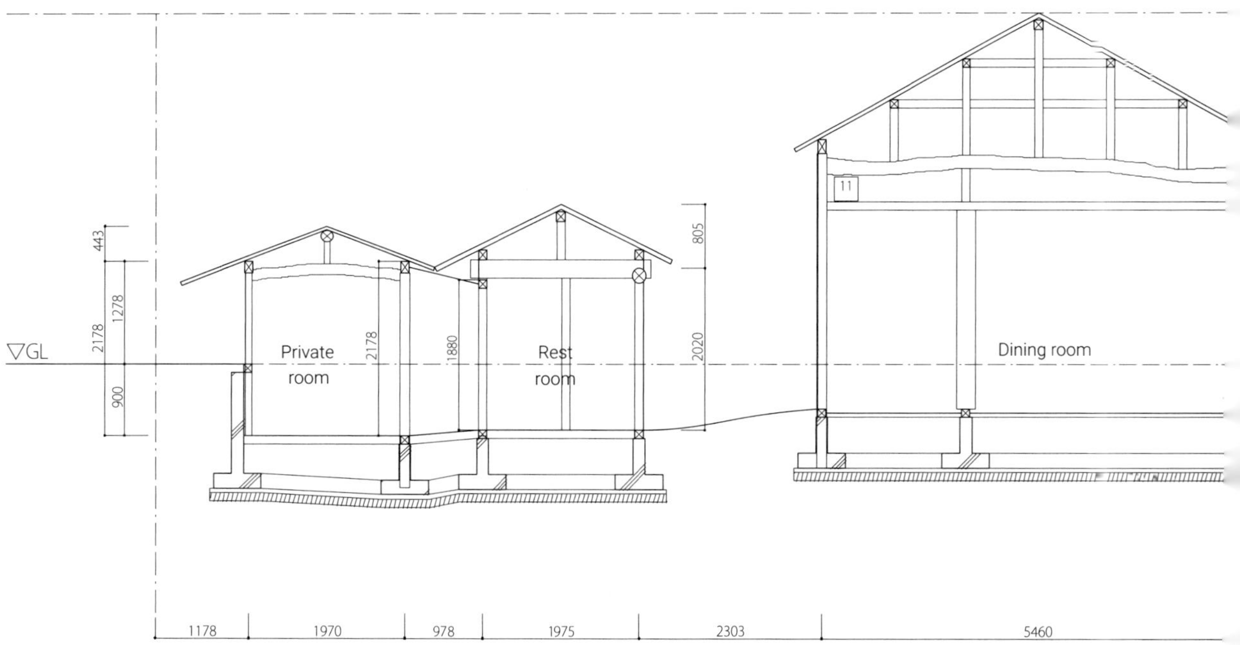
443
1278
2178
900
▽GL
Private room
2178
1880
Rest room
805
2020
11
Dining room
1178
1970
978
1975
2303
5460

Sections

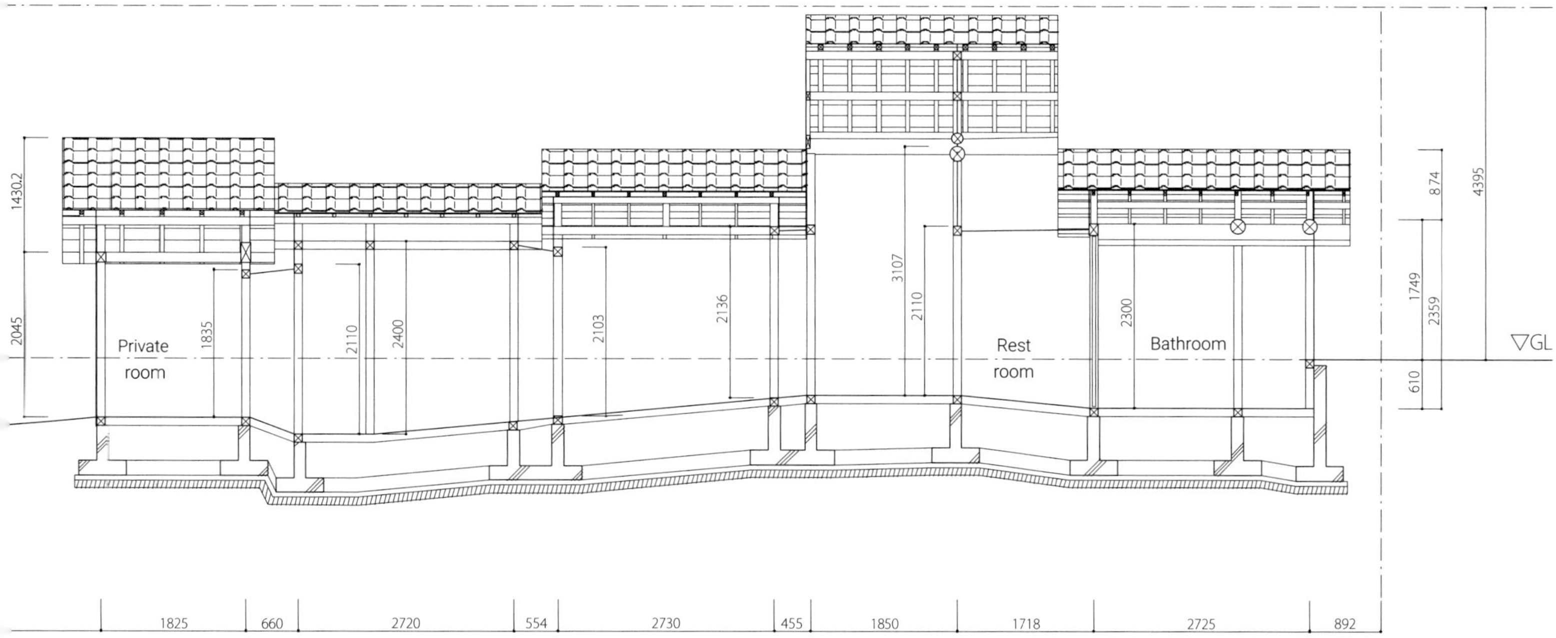

1430.2
2045
Private
room
1835
2110
2400
2103
2136
3107
2110
Rest
room
2300
Bathroom
874
1749
2359
610
4395
▽GL
1825
660
2720
554
2730
455
1850
1718
2725
892

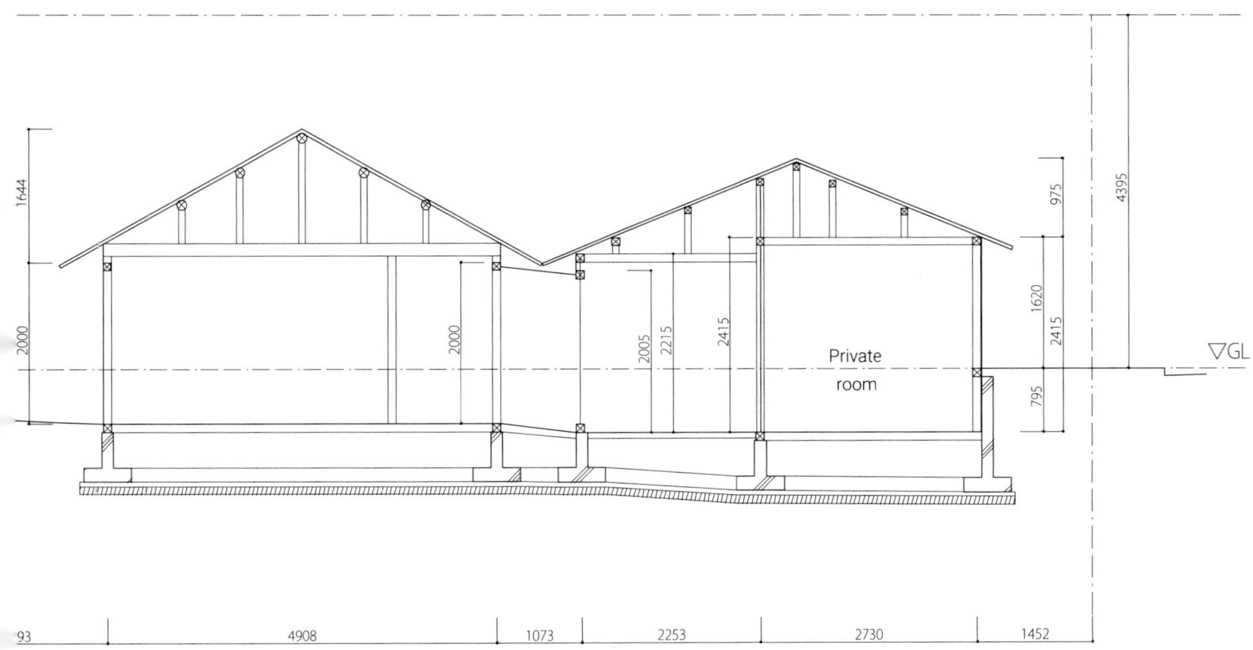

1644
2000
2000
2005
2215
2415
Private
room
975
1620
2415
795
4395
▽GL
93
4908
1073
2253
2730
1452

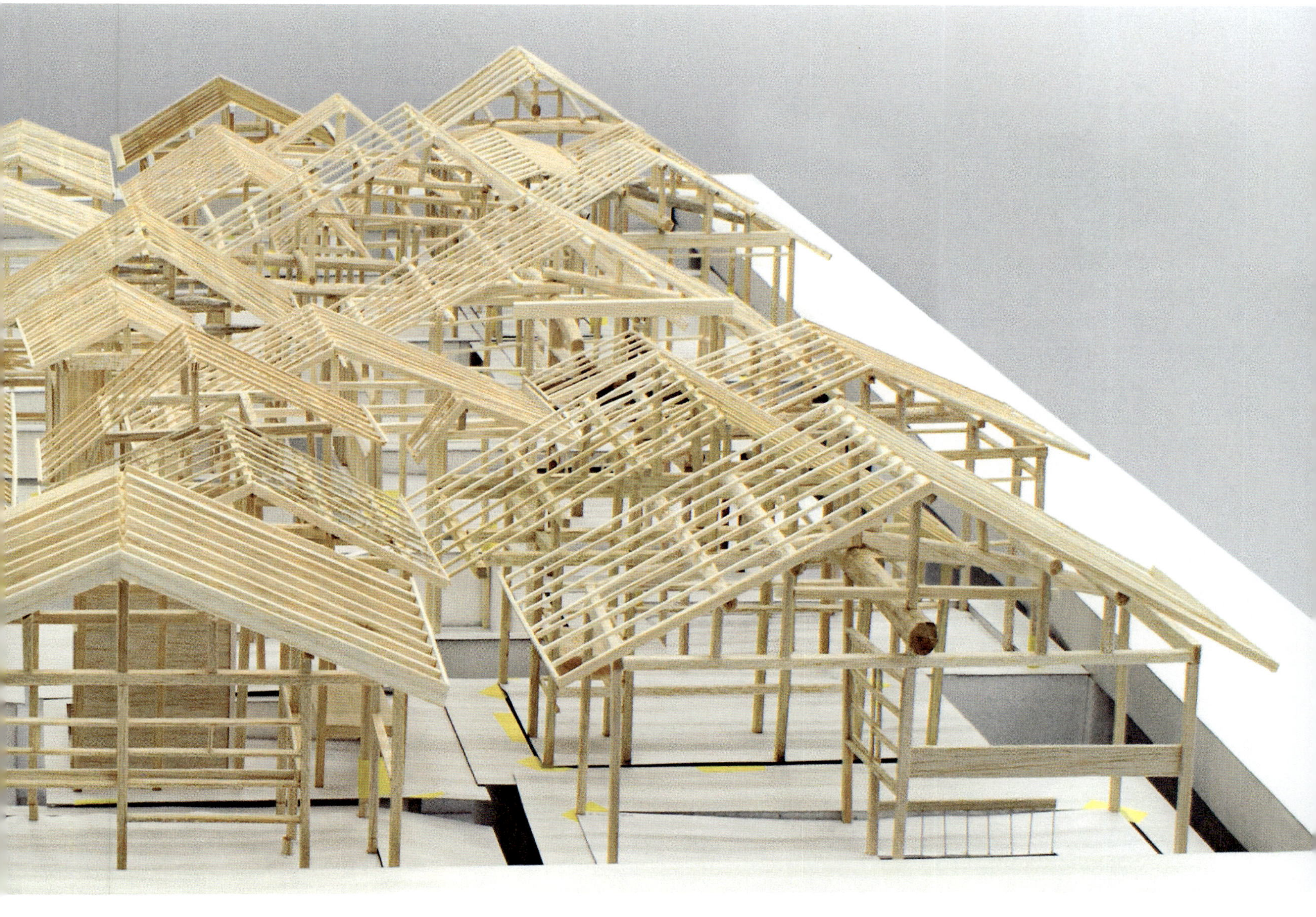

Botanical Garden Art Biotop / Water Garden, Tochigi

2013-2018

The objective of this project was to create a rental farm and garden in the surrounding site of a hotel that stands within the beautiful natural area of Nasu, in Tochigi Prefecture. Even though it is a rental farm, its concept is not concerned simply with the leasing of land allotments. Visitors share the garden-like space with others as they plant crops in the fields, gather fruits and nuts, or cook their harvests at the hotel. Our aim was to harness activities that are associated with nature within the context of existing culture.

The existing site was almost flat and had previously been a meadow. In proceeding with this project I believed that we needed to think about the geometry and the repetition of existing farms in a manner different to that of a common farm plan. The scenery that farms create is seemingly more artificial and automatic than any city in the world. The efficiency required for increasing the amount of crops is prioritized above anything else. However, in this project the most important concern was how humans are able to create things that can be a part of the existing scenery, and how those who visit can feel relaxed and at ease. In this beautiful scenery, people experience and learn about the natural environment; understanding the process from growing to cooking and eating the crops. The entire process takes place within this very space. Additionally, since there had been a demand for a diverse variety of agricultural produce, it was necessary to plant as many crops as possible that can be switched and repositioned within a small area. On the basis of such interests, I intended to create a landscape with a small environment of vegetation that is in a state of ever-changing flux, like a kaleidoscope. What I aimed to achieve in this project is to realize a *dream-like landscape*.

Instead of the standard geometry of farms, which are based on straight lines, I specifically designed the site plan with a geometric pattern conceived through a complicated arrangement of curvatures like the repetition of puzzle pieces. The soil was dug up in certain areas to make ponds. The ground is designed to be both garden and farm, and is an environment that can be used by people. The ponds are designed as space that is not meant for people, and takes on the role of shaping the structure of the whole farm. With the shape of the new ground itself designating its 'structure,' the beautiful scenery containing various crops is maintained. Countless small gardens emerge in the space between the ponds. This level of scale is designed like that of the Japanese courtyard garden of *tsubo-niwa*. We aim to transform the scale of that which is familiar to people into the much larger scale of the natural environment.

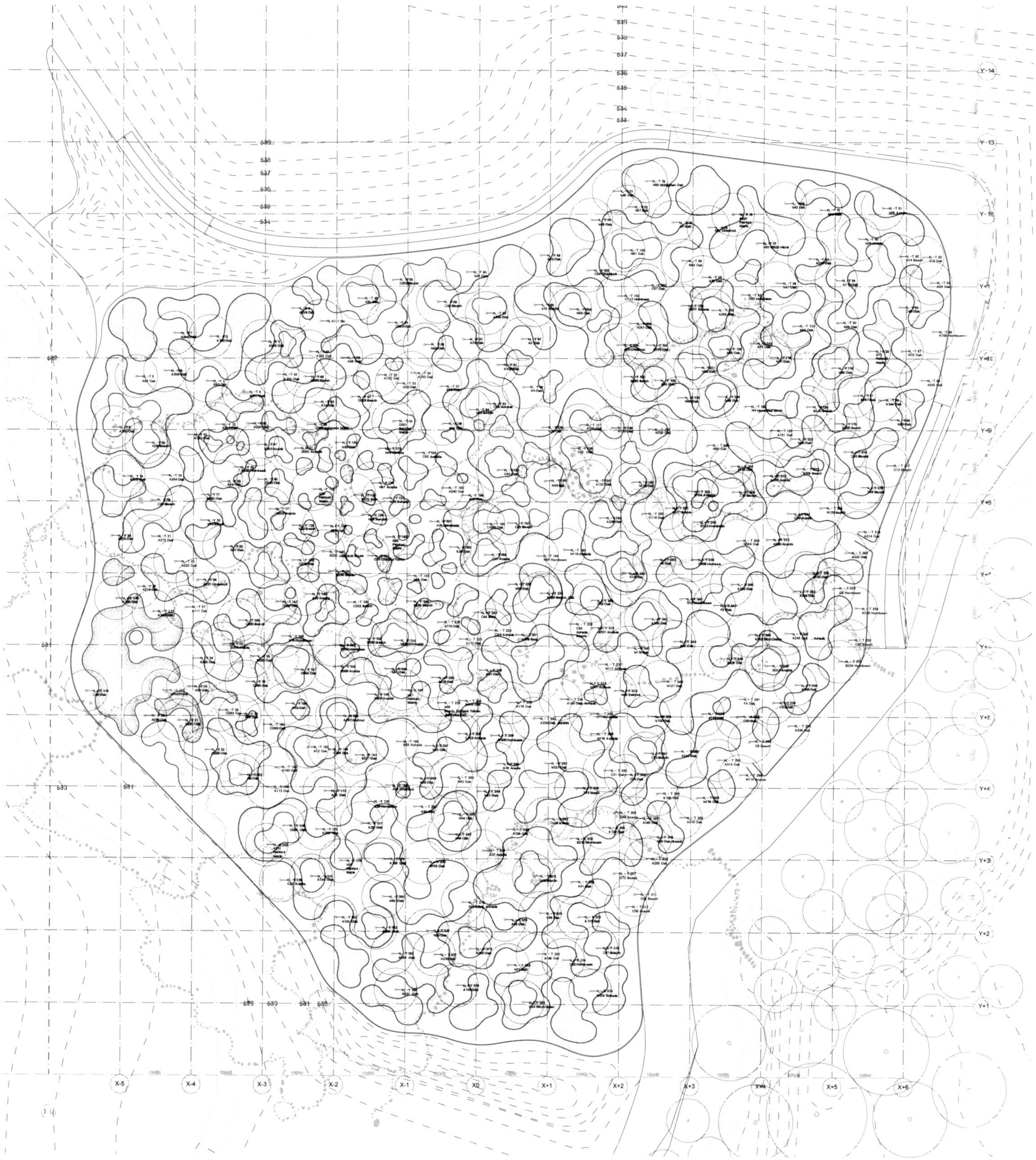

Ground plan

N114
Acacia
H=16m
Φ=260
P=980mm
C6
Beech
Entrance
Rubber Band
Assorted Moss
Improved Soil
Existing Earth
Roadbed
Crusheran
Roadbed
Design CBR≥3
Field Soil Covering
Root Ball
L-Shaped Angle
A93
H=13m
Φ=270mm
P=990mm
X+4 Section
NºP2
Lv - 532.95
▽Water Level
Water Level - 0.10
Water Level - 0.20
Water Level - 0.30
Stepping Stone
Discrete Concrete
NºP4
Lv - 532.90
▽Water Level
Water Level - 0.10
Water Level - 0.20
Water Level - 0.30
Stepping Stone
Foundation Stones
Levelling Concrete
Rubber Band
Field Soil Covering
Bentonite Waterproofing Sheet
Field Soil Covering
Root Ball
L-Shaped Angle
X-4 Section
A32
H=14m
Φ=300mm
P=1100mm
Assorted Moss
Improved Soil
NºP106
Lv - 532.80
▽Water Level
Water Level - 0.10
Drainage Pipe Φ100
(Overflow Wastewater)
Assorted Moss
Improved Soil 100
NºP106
Lv - 532.80
▽Water Level
Water Level - 0.10
Water Level - 0.20
Water Level - 0.30
Water Level - 0.40
Existing Earth
Field Soil Covering
Bentonite Waterproofing Sheet
Main Pipe Φ250
X+2 Section
Stepping Stone
Levelling Concrete
Drainage Pipe Φ100
(Overflow Wastewater)
NºP25
Lv - 533.00
▽Water Level
Water Level - 0.10
Water Level - 0.20
Drainage Pipe Φ100
(Overflow Wastewater)
Bench
Field Soil Covering
Bentonite Waterproofing Sheet
X+3 Section
N81
H=16m
Φ=260mm
P=980mm
NºP98
Lv - 532.55
Drainage Pipe Φ100
(Overflow Wastewater)
Rubber Band
NºP99
Lv - 532.60
▽Water Level
Water Level - 0.10
Water Level - 0.20
Water Level - 0.30
Communication Pipe
Siphon Type
VUΦ100
Trickle Pipe
Φ100
NºP100
Lv - 532.65
▽Water Level
Water Level - 0.10
Water Level - 0.20
Field Soil Covering
Bentonite Waterproofing Sheet
Field Soil Covering
Field Soil Covering
Bentonite Waterproofing Sheet
Field Soil Covering
Bentonite Waterproofing Sheet
Root Ball
L-Shaped Angle
X-1 Section

Sections

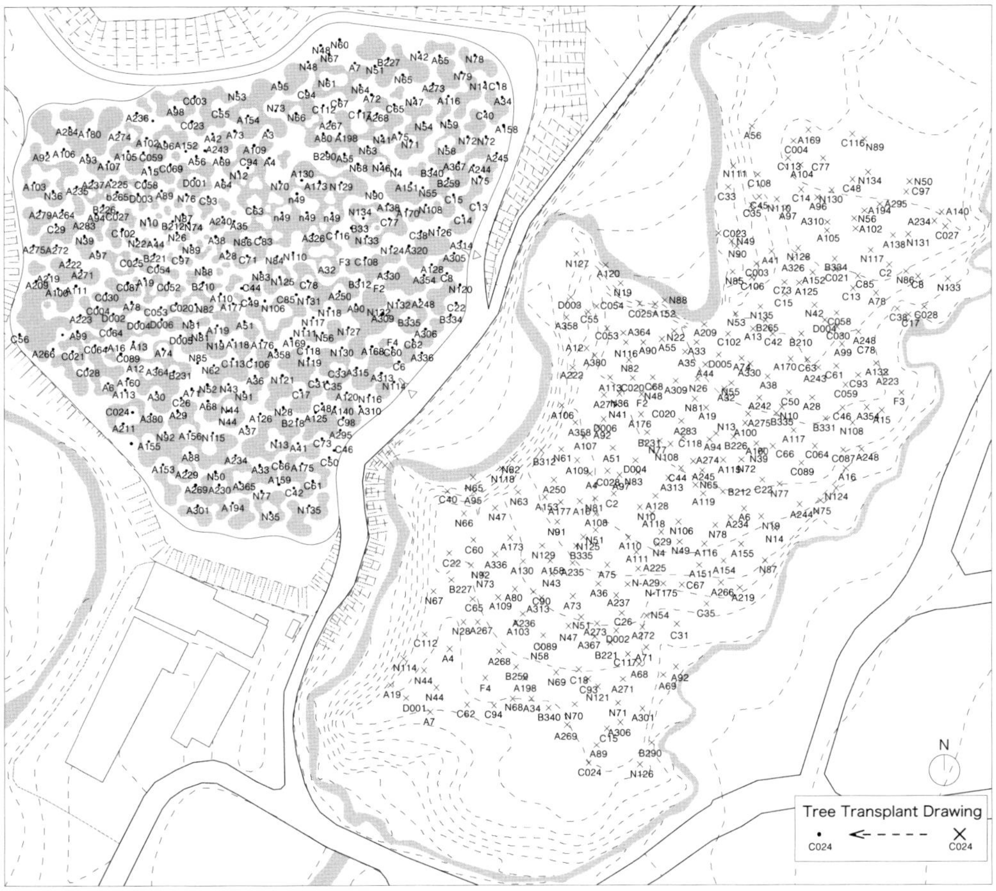
Tree Transplant Drawing
C024
C024
N

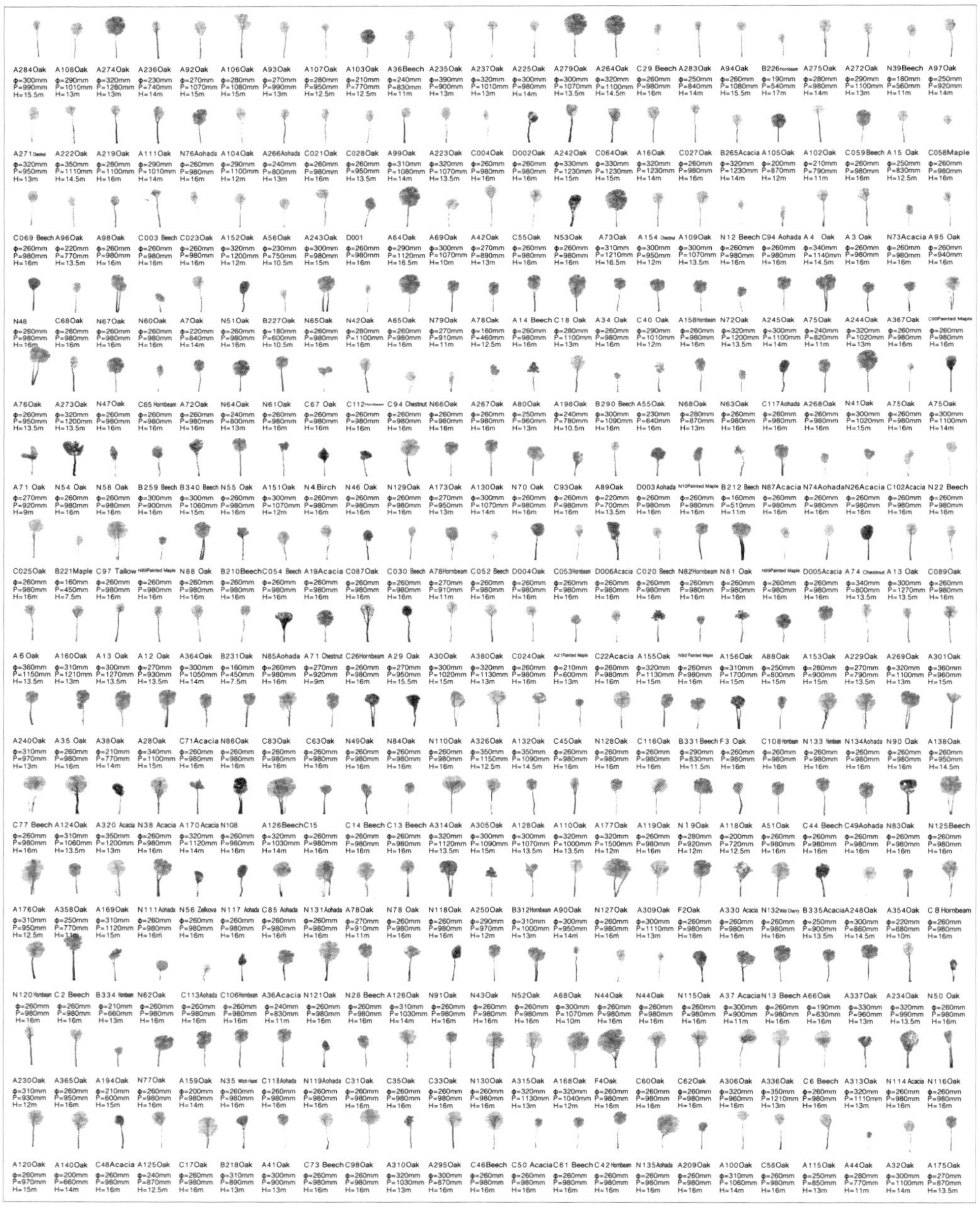

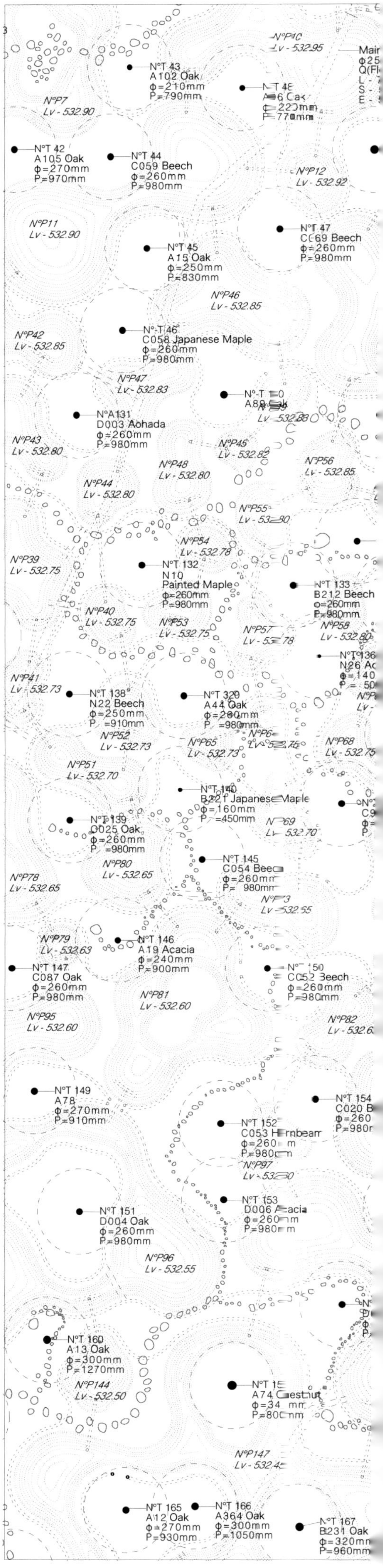
N°T 43
A102 Oak
ϕ=210mm
P=790mm
N°P7
Lv - 532.90
N°T 42
A105 Oak
ϕ=270mm
P=970mm
N°T 44
C059 Beech
ϕ=260mm
P=980mm
N°P12
Lv - 532.92
N°P11
Lv - 532.90
N°T 45
A15 Oak
ϕ=250mm
P=830mm
N°T 47
C069 Beech
ϕ=260mm
P=980mm
N°P46
Lv - 532.85
N°P42
Lv - 532.85
C058 Japanese Maple
ϕ=260mm
P=980mm
N°P47
Lv - 532.83
N°A131
D003 Aohada
ϕ=260mm
P=980mm
N°P43
Lv - 532.80
N°P48
Lv - 532.80
N°P44
Lv - 532.80
N°P56
Lv - 532.85
N°P54
Lv - 532.78
N°P39
Lv - 532.75
N°T 132
N10
Painted Maple
ϕ=260mm
P=980mm
N°T 133
B212 Beech
N°P40
Lv - 532.75
N°P53
Lv - 532.75
N°P41
Lv - 532.73
N°T 138
N22 Beech
ϕ=250mm
P=910mm
N°T 329
A44 Oak
N°P52
Lv - 532.73
N°P65
Lv - 532.73
N°P68
Lv - 532.75
N°P51
Lv - 532.70
B221 Japanese Maple
ϕ=160mm
P=450mm
N°T 139
C025 Oak
ϕ=260mm
P=980mm
N°T 145
C054 Beech
N°P80
Lv - 532.65
N°P78
Lv - 532.65
N°P79
Lv - 532.63
N°T 146
A19 Acacia
ϕ=240mm
P=900mm
N°T 147
C087 Oak
ϕ=260mm
P=980mm
N°P81
Lv - 532.60
N°P95
Lv - 532.60
N°T 149
A78
ϕ=270mm
P=910mm
N°T 154
N°T 151
D004 Oak
ϕ=260mm
P=980mm
N°P96
Lv - 532.55
N°T 160
A13 Oak
ϕ=300mm
P=1270mm
N°P144
Lv - 532.50
N°P147
N°T 165
A12 Oak
ϕ=270mm
P=930mm
N°T 166
A364 Oak
ϕ=300mm
P=1050mm
N°T 167
B231 Oak
ϕ=320mm
P=960mm

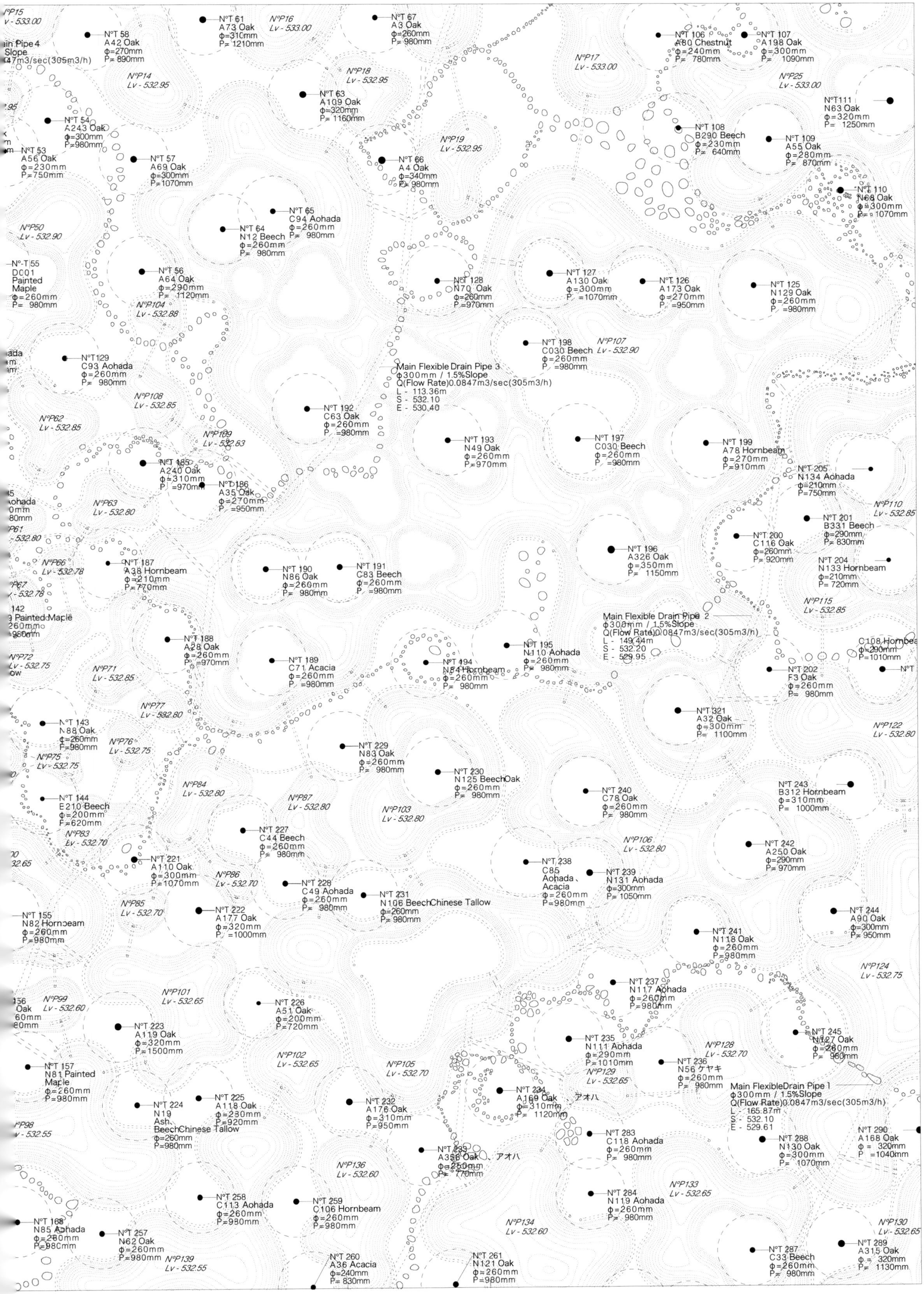

N°P15 Lv - 533.00
N°T 61 A73 Oak ϕ=310mm P= 1210mm
N°P16 Lv - 533.00
N°T 67 A3 Oak ϕ=260mm P= 980mm
N°T 106 A80 Chestnut ϕ=240mm P= 780mm
N°T 107 A198 Oak ϕ=300mm P= 1090mm
N°T 58 A42 Oak ϕ=270mm P= 890mm
ain Pipe 4 Slope 47m3/sec(305m3/h)
N°P17 Lv - 533.00
N°P18 Lv - 532.95
N°P14 Lv - 532.95
N°P25 Lv - 533.00
N°T 63 A109 Oak ϕ=320mm P= 1160mm
N°T111 N63 Oak ϕ=320mm P= 1250mm
N°T 54 A243 Oak ϕ=300mm P=980mm
N°T 108 B290 Beech ϕ=230mm P= 640mm
N°T 109 A55 Oak ϕ=280mm P= 870mm
N°P19 Lv - 532.95
N°T 53 A56 Oak ϕ=230mm P=750mm
N°T 57 A69 Oak ϕ=300mm P=1070mm
N°T 66 A4 Oak ϕ=340mm P= 980mm
N°T 110 N68 Oak ϕ=300mm P= 1070mm
N°T 65 C94 Aohada ϕ=260mm P= 980mm
N°T 64 N12 Beech ϕ=260mm P= 980mm
N°P50 Lv - 532.90
N°T 55 DC01 Painted Maple ϕ=260mm P= 980mm
N°T 56 A64 Oak ϕ=290mm P= 1120mm
N°T 128 N70 Oak ϕ=260mm P=970mm
N°T 127 A130 Oak ϕ=300mm P =1070mm
N°T 126 A173 Oak ϕ=270mm P =950mm
N°T 125 N129 Oak ϕ=260mm P =980mm
N°P104 Lv - 532.88
N°T 198 C030 Beech ϕ=260mm P =980mm
N°P107 Lv - 532.90
N°T129 C93 Aohada ϕ=260mm P= 980mm
Main Flexible Drain Pipe 3 ϕ300mm / 1.5%Slope Q(Flow Rate)0.0847m3/sec(305m3/h) L - 113.36m S - 532.10 E - 530.40
N°P108 Lv - 532.85
N°T 192 C63 Oak ϕ=260mm P =980mm
N°P62 Lv - 532.85
N°T 193 N49 Oak ϕ=260mm P=970mm
N°T 197 C030 Beech ϕ=260mm P =980mm
N°T 199 A78 Hornbeam ϕ=270mm P=910mm
N°P109 Lv - 532.83
N°T 185 A240 Oak ϕ=310mm P =970mm
N°T 186 A35 Oak ϕ=270mm P =950mm
N°T 205 N134 Aohada ϕ=210mm P=750mm
N°P63 Lv - 532.80
N°P110 Lv - 532.85
N°T 201 B331 Beech ϕ=290mm P= 830mm
N°T 200 C116 Oak ϕ=260mm P= 920mm
N°T 196 A326 Oak ϕ=350mm P= 1150mm
N°T 204 N133 Hornbeam ϕ=210mm P= 720mm
N°P61 Lv - 532.80
N°P66 Lv - 532.78
N°T 187 A38 Hornbeam ϕ=210mm P=770mm
N°T 190 N86 Oak ϕ=260mm P= 980mm
N°T 191 C83 Beech ϕ=260mm P =980mm
N°P67 Lv - 532.78
142 Painted Maple 260mm 980mm
N°P115 Lv - 532.85
Main Flexible Drain Pipe 2 ϕ300mm / 1.5%Slope Q(Flow Rate)0.0847m3/sec(305m3/h) L - 149.44m S - 532.20 E - 529.95
N°T 188 A28 Oak ϕ=260mm P =970mm
N°T 195 N110 Aohada ϕ=260mm P= 980mm
C108 Hornbea ϕ=290mm P=1010mm
N°P72 Lv - 532.75
N°T 189 C71 Acacia ϕ=260mm P =980mm
N°T 194 N84 Hornbeam ϕ=260mm P= 980mm
N°T 202 F3 Oak ϕ=260mm P= 980mm
N°P71 Lv - 532.85
N°P77 Lv - 532.80
N°T 321 A32 Oak ϕ=300mm P= 1100mm
N°T 143 N88 Oak ϕ=260mm P=980mm
N°P76 Lv - 532.75
N°T 229 N83 Oak ϕ=260mm P= 980mm
N°P122 Lv - 532.80
N°P75 Lv - 532.75
N°T 230 N125 BeechOak ϕ=260mm P= 980mm
N°P84 Lv - 532.80
N°T 240 C78 Oak ϕ=260mm P= 980mm
N°T 243 B312 Hornbeam ϕ=310mm P= 1000mm
N°T 144 E210 Beech ϕ=200mm P=620mm
N°P87 Lv - 532.80
N°P103 Lv - 532.80
N°T 227 C44 Beech ϕ=260mm P= 980mm
N°P106 Lv - 532.80
N°T 242 A250 Oak ϕ=290mm P= 970mm
N°P83 Lv - 532.70
N°T 221 A110 Oak ϕ=300mm P=1070mm
N°T 238 C85 Aohada、Acacia ϕ=260mm P=980mm
N°T 239 N131 Aohada ϕ=300mm P= 1050mm
N°P86 Lv - 532.70
N°T 228 C49 Aohada ϕ=260mm P= 980mm
N°T 231 N106 BeechChinese Tallow ϕ=260mm P= 980mm
N°P85 Lv - 532.70
N°T 222 A177 Oak ϕ=320mm P =1000mm
N°T 155 N82 Hornbeam ϕ=260mm P=980mm
N°T 244 A90 Oak ϕ=300mm P= 950mm
N°T 241 N118 Oak ϕ=260mm P=980mm
N°P124 Lv - 532.75
N°T 237 N117 Aohada ϕ=260mm P=980mm
N°P101 Lv - 532.65
N°P99 Lv - 532.60
N°T 226 A51 Oak ϕ=200mm P=720mm
N°T 223 A119 Oak ϕ=320mm P= 1500mm
N°T 235 N111 Aohada ϕ=290mm P=1010mm
N°T 245 N127 Oak ϕ=260mm P= 980mm
N°P128 Lv - 532.70
N°P102 Lv - 532.65
N°P105 Lv - 532.70
N°T 236 N56 ケヤキ ϕ=260mm P= 980mm
N°P129 Lv - 532.65
N°T 157 N81 Painted Maple ϕ=260mm P=980mm
Main FlexibleDrain Pipe 1 ϕ300mm / 1.5%Slope Q(Flow Rate)0.0847m3/sec(305m3/h) L - 165.87m S - 532.10 E - 529.61
N°T 225 A118 Oak ϕ=280mm P=920mm
N°T 234 A169 Oak、アオハ ϕ=310mm P= 1120mm
N°T 224 N19 Ash BeechChinese Tallow ϕ=260mm P=980mm
N°T 232 A176 Oak ϕ=310mm P=950mm
N°P98 Lv - 532.55
N°T 283 C118 Aohada ϕ=260mm P= 980mm
N°T 290 A168 Oak ϕ= 320mm P =1040mm
N°T 288 N130 Oak ϕ=300mm P= 1070mm
N°T 233 A336 Oak 、アオハ ϕ=250mm P= 770mm
N°P136 Lv - 532.60
N°P133 Lv - 532.65
N°T 258 C113 Aohada ϕ=260mm P=980mm
N°T 259 C106 Hornbeam ϕ=260mm P=980mm
N°T 284 N119 Aohada ϕ=260mm P= 980mm
N°P130 Lv - 532.65
N°T 168 N85 Aohada ϕ=260mm P=980mm
N°T 257 N62 Oak ϕ=260mm P=980mm
N°P134 Lv - 532.60
N°T 289 A315 Oak ϕ= 320mm P= 1130mm
N°T 287 C33 Beech ϕ=260mm P= 980mm
N°P139 Lv - 532.55
N°T 260 A36 Acacia ϕ=240mm P= 830mm
N°T 261 N121 Oak ϕ=260mm P=980mm

House and restaurant, Yamaguchi

2013-

This project consists of a house and a restaurant for the same owner, a chef, who wanted a cave-like space as a bodega. To that end it was necessary to dig a series of wells or craters in the ground, some of them interconnected, others not, and then to pour concrete into the holes. Once dried and removed from the earth surrounding it, the concrete mass constitutes the structure of the building, a concrete volume that looks like a rock, and which, after positioning the outer walls, turns into an architecture and a landscape of variegated forms. It casts the shade of the earth and the stones on the site. The unexpected forms and curves of the walls born from this "inverted" fabrication technique imitate those of a cave. Three inner courtyards separate the living space from the restaurant. Plate glass provides discreet openings onto the exterior vegetation, permitting the natural light to filter through, thereby creating a building that could be paradoxically classified as a sun-filled cave.Visitors accede to the restaurant via a small entrance before arriving at a room with a large opening with views of the outside where they can enjoy the food and conversation. The living area is made up of seemingly random spaces full of light, which enters from the exterior windows and interior patios.

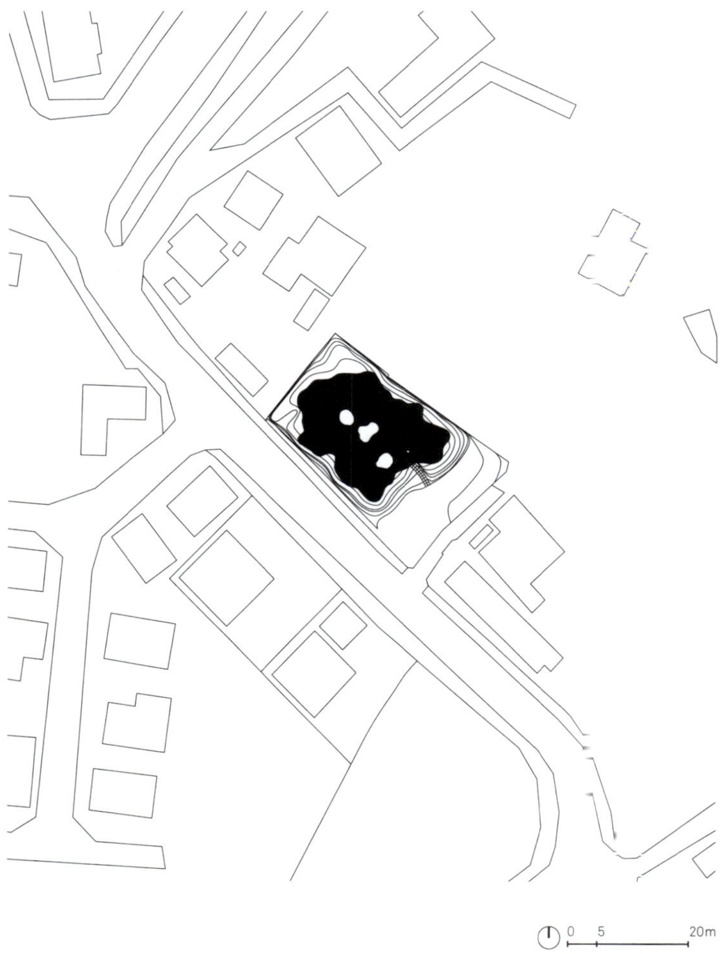

Concept drawings

terrace
dining room
courtyard
closet
shelf
bedroom
kitchen
refrigerator
living room
washing machine
rooftop GL=+44

Floor plan

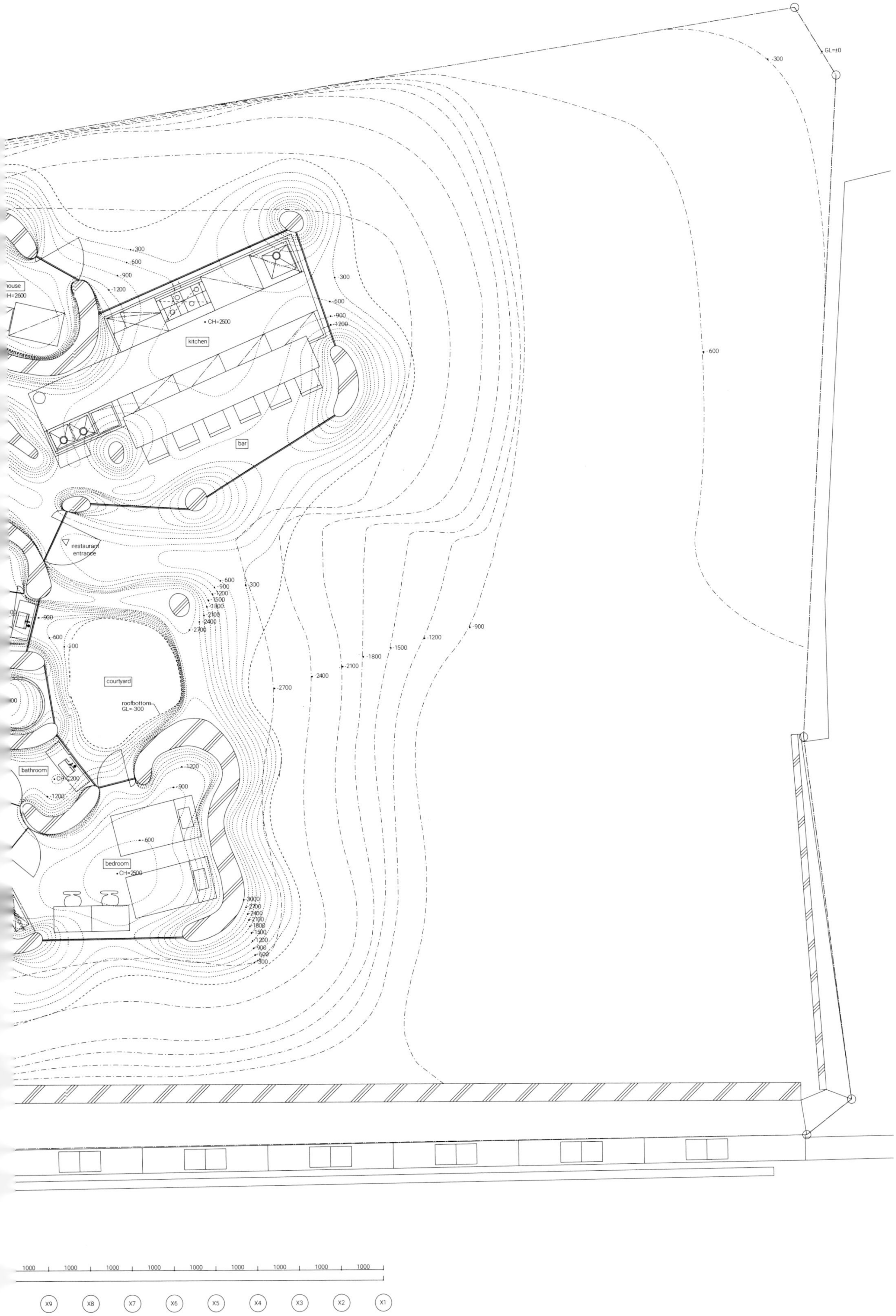
kitchen
bar
restaurant entrance
courtyard
roofbottom GL=-300
bathroom
bedroom
CH=2500
GL=±0

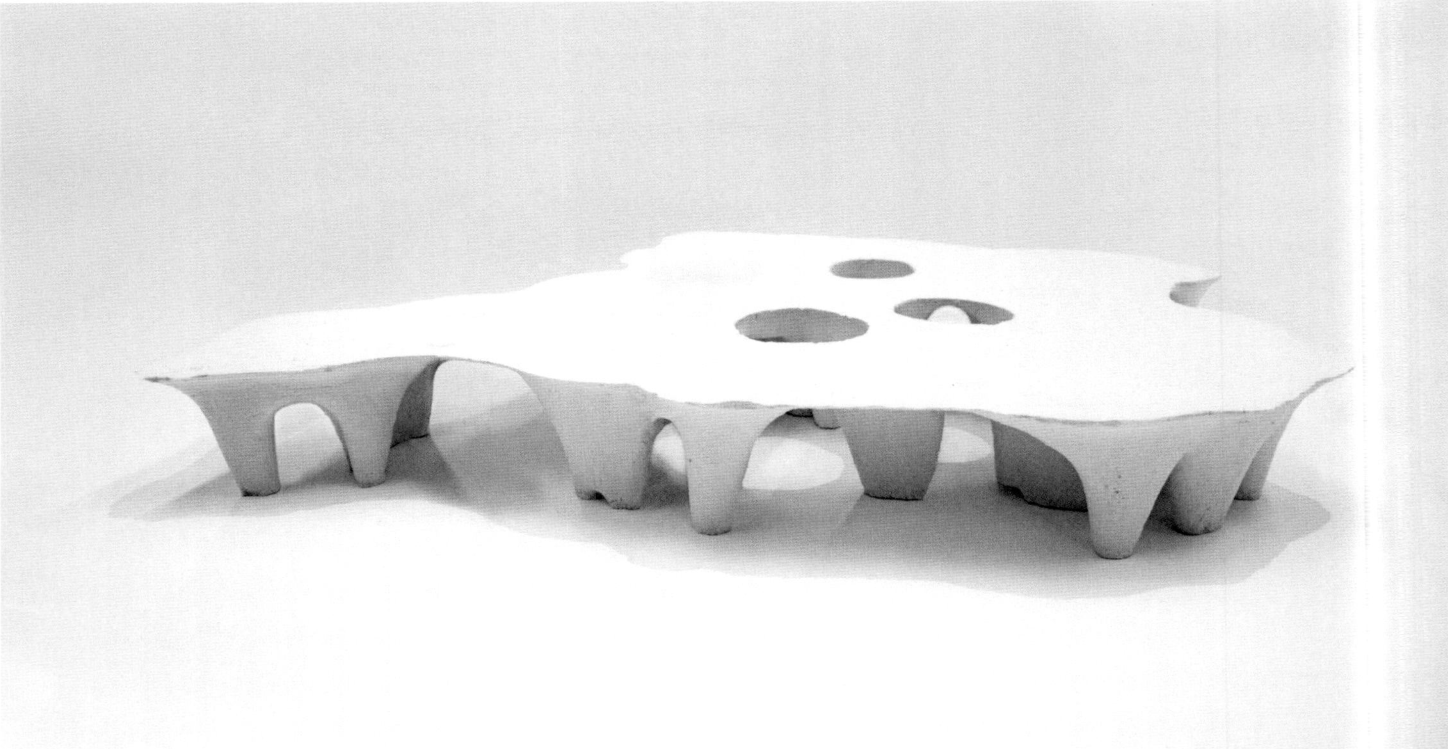

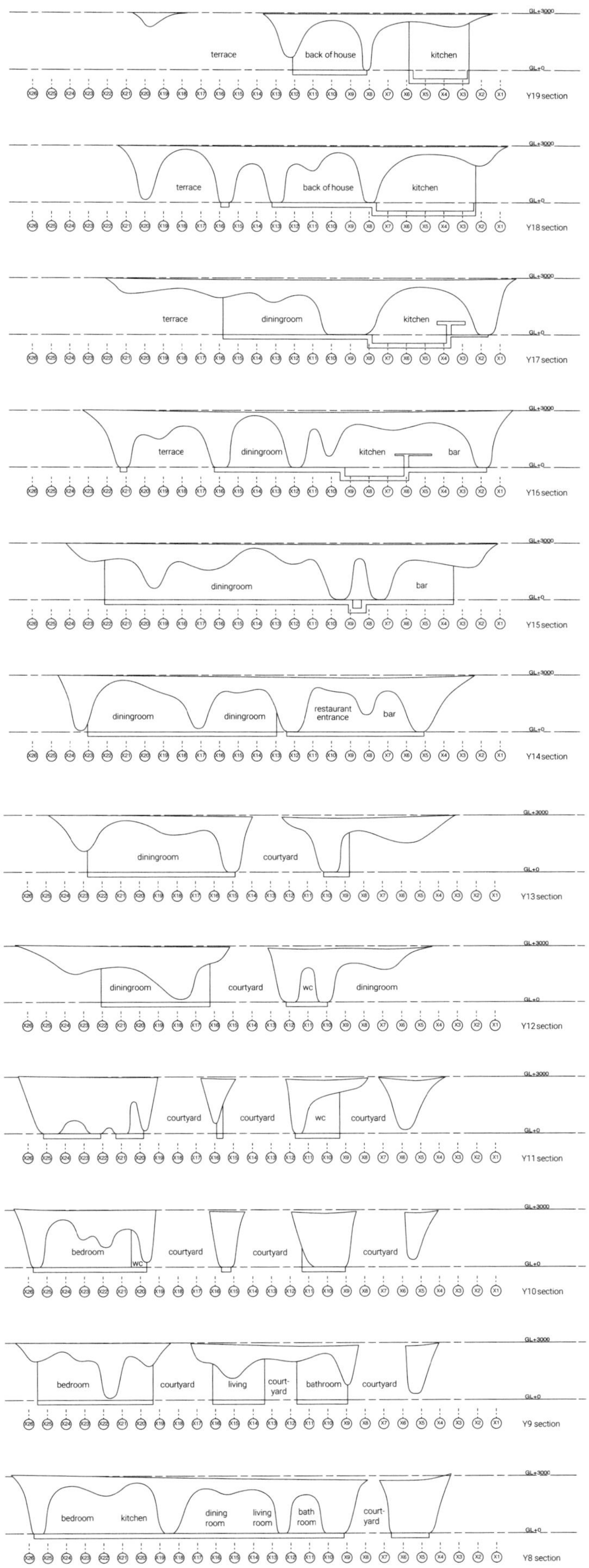
terrace
back of house
kitchen
Y19 section
terrace
back of house
kitchen
Y18 section
terrace
diningroom
kitchen
Y17 section
terrace
diningroom
kitchen
bar
Y16 section
diningroom
bar
Y15 section
diningroom
diningroom
restaurant entrance
bar
Y14 section
diningroom
courtyard
Y13 section
diningroom
courtyard
wc
diningroom
Y12 section
courtyard
courtyard
wc
courtyard
Y11 section
bedroom
wc
courtyard
courtyard
courtyard
Y10 section
bedroom
courtyard
living
court-yard
bathroom
courtyard
Y9 section
bedroom
kitchen
dining room
living room
bath room
court-yard
Y8 section

Sections

Family house

2013-

This is a residence planned for Junya Ishigami's parents and grandmother, on the site where his grandmother's current house stands. Aging and in need of rebuilding, this house was the architect's first home, on a corner that was once a rural village. The design is guided by his memory of the place and the scenery: the horizontal paddy fields stretching into the distance, the large south-oriented garden always in view from the house, a spacious *tatami* room expanding the interior. This variety of existing scenery is gathered together to compose the spaces of the new house. Covered by a shed roof curving lightly downwards, the boundless *tatami* room and the large southern garden are connected as a single continuous surface to make an expanse of horizontal scenery. A low wall encloses the garden, where the trees that have long been present on the site are retained. Small plants grow on the curved roof, with eaves below the line of vision so that roof and ground become a single continuous garden embracing the site, surrounded by hedges and windbreak trees. These elements obscure the newly constructed neighboring houses, which differ from the existing village scenery. The view of the south garden fills a very long, low window 1.3 m high and 25 m long. Blending into the neighborhood, the low wall merges with the existing hedge at about head height, with views of the tall tree next door, the paddy fields spreading beyond, and the mountains in the distance. The house is an expansive structure composed of present-day scenery and the scenery of memory, merged to form a continuous living space at the scale of both the site and the inhabitants.

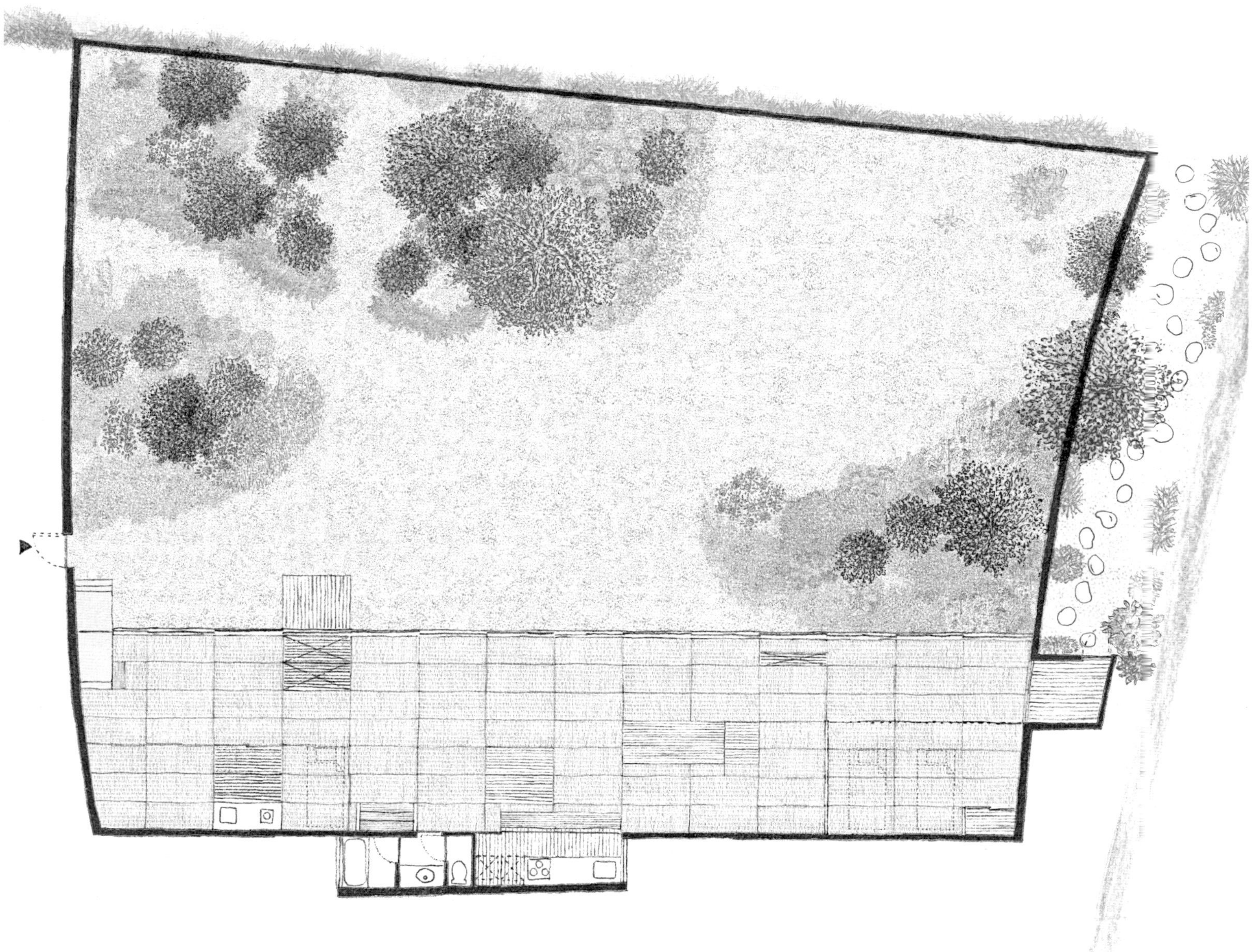

Floor plan

Forest kindergarten, Shandong

2015-

This kindergarten is situated in a densely forested area in the countryside of Shandong, China. The project intends to create an architecture to connect children with their surrounding natural environment and to reflect perspectives from their world. The idea was to plan the spatial composition of the building as little as possible to allow for freedom in the children's play and activities. Most of the space is designed at children's scale, but a range of architectural scales was considered to think about the different spaces: classrooms include the scale of an adult, other spaces can only be used by children, still others are places where even children crawling or crouching cannot reach, so that every space inspires a multitude of activities. A reinforced-concrete roof with large openings covers the building and merges with the ground in many places, creating spaces for play and other activities. The roof is supported on slender steel pillars, which transfer the vertical load, while the horizontal load is carried by the contact points with the ground. The design of the roof follows a process of study through a series of collages, each gathering images such as animals, plants, and children's illustrations. These studies are progressively stylized to create the shape and contours of the building.

Emerging from no longer recognizable figurative imagery, the architecture uses form to allow children to perceive and imagine a multitude of visions and possibilities. For instance, where the roof dips downward, children feel as if they are falling on top of a flower or sliding down an elephant's trunk. Abstract and concrete, giant and minuscule, interior and exterior combine so that each space gives each child the possibility to explore the infinity of his or her imagination, thereby creating an architecture made entirely out of non-architectural elements. This architecture is designed as a landscape made of children scales and unique way of seeing the world.

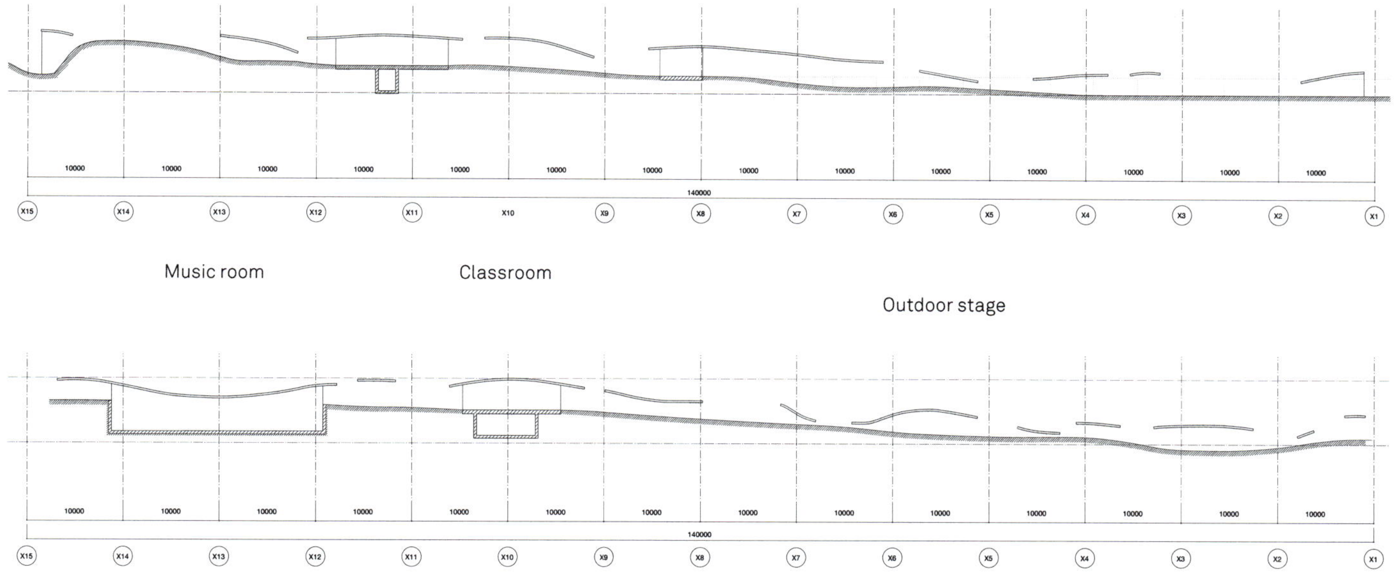

Sections

Parents
Soatry
Running
Court
Seating
Terrace
Roof
Play
Swings
Play
Classroom
Waterfall
&
Droplets
Holes
Play
Rain
Music
Room
Echo Room
Bar
Play
Running
Bridge
Ladder
Play
Classroom
Outdoor
Amphiteatre
Rope Swing
Resting
Wall
Hill
Play
Slider
Classroom
Low
Terrace
Plants
Corner
Terrace
Climbing
Wall
Mole
House
Water
Garden
Swing

Floor plan

View Terrace
Swing
Column Play
Terrace
Slider
Rain Room
Classroom
Nursery
Terrace
Open Courtyard
Nursery
Rain
Small Terrace
Swing
Table
Outdoor Room
Amphitheatre
Swing
Sliding Hill
Swing Yarol
Swing
Outdoor Stage
Outdoor Room
Dark Room
Playing Net
Pond Courtyard
Ladder Climb
Sliding Roof
Long run
Doctor Room
Outdoor Play
Low Room
Classroom
Climbing Wall
Roof Terrace
Slider
Play Hill
Rain Roof
Main Entrance
Swing
Outdoor Room
Pond Garden
Colomn Play
Circle Swing
Outdoor Classroom
Terrace
Swing
Ropenet Playground
Column Play
Run Bridge
Touch Room
0 1
20 m

TUNNEL

Chapel of the Valley, Shandong

2016-

Chapel of the Valley is an ecumenical chapel located at the bottom of a very small valley in Shandong, China. The project takes advantage of the terrain's natural ruggedness. Accentuating the depth of the crevices by approximately 20 m, the chapel literally seems to surge forth from the ground. The building rises to a height of 45 m with a width of 1.3 m at its narrowest part. The chapel consists of two closely spaced reinforced-concrete curving walls, varying from 22 to 180 cm in thickness. The walls, which run alongside each other to form a narrow entrance, gradually move further apart, then merge to enclose the altar space. Because space gets wider as one moves forward in the building, the entrance is plunged into darkness while the altar receives sunlight. Therefore, this space sequence creates the impression that light comes from the depth of the building. The chapel space is a continuation of the existing valley, though its scale radically exceeds that of the existing landscape; a new valley is created, open to the wind and rain.

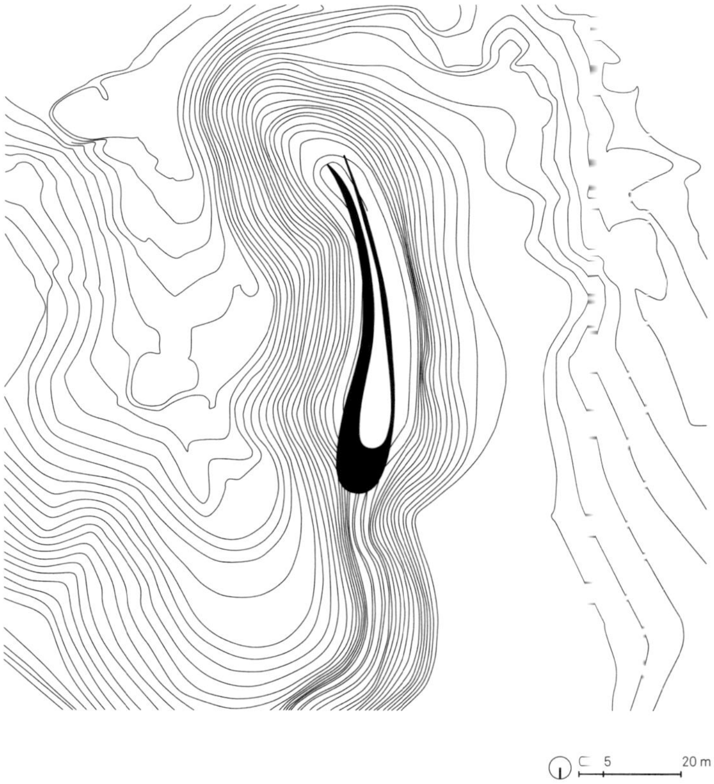

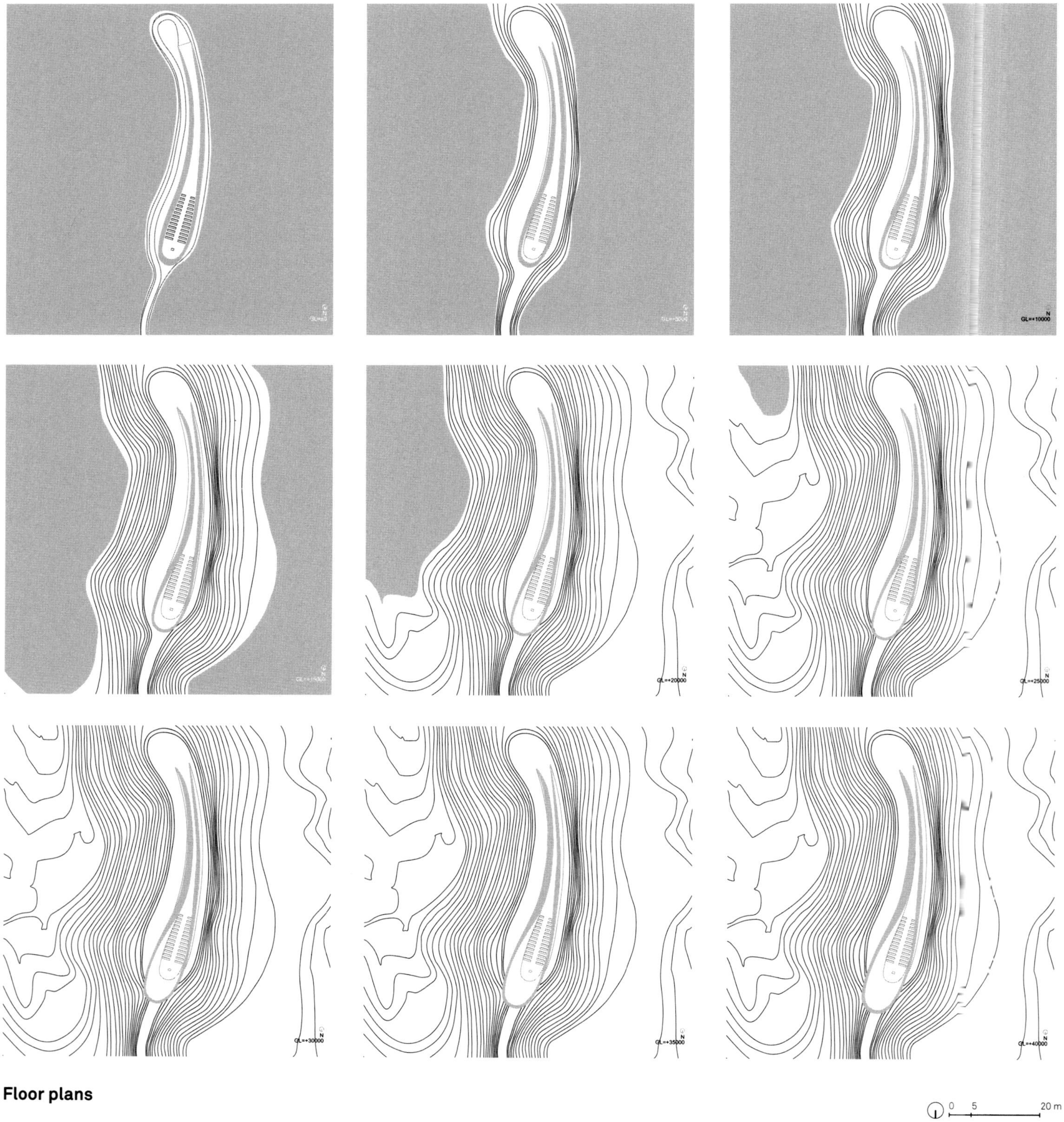

Floor plans

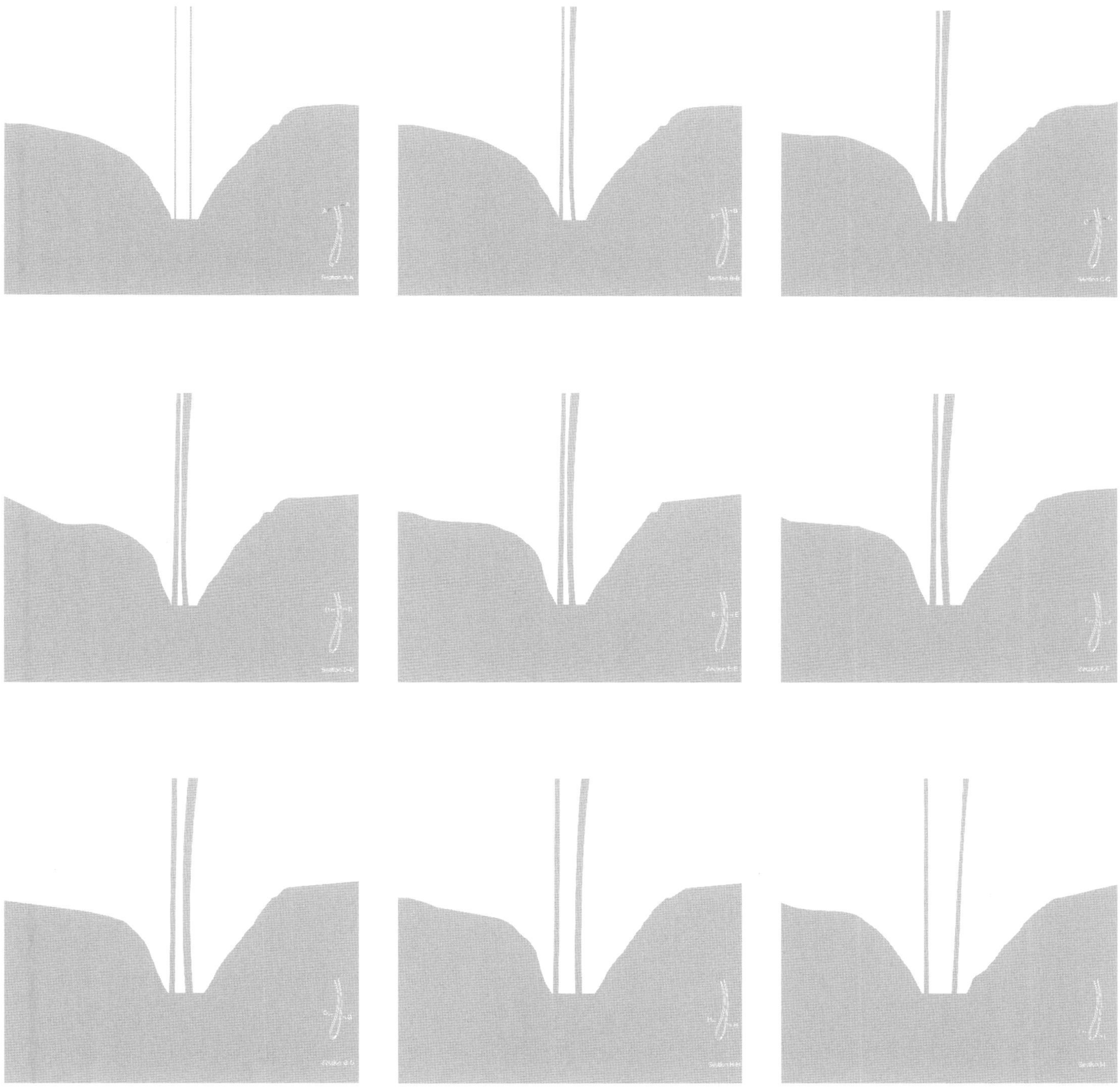

Sections

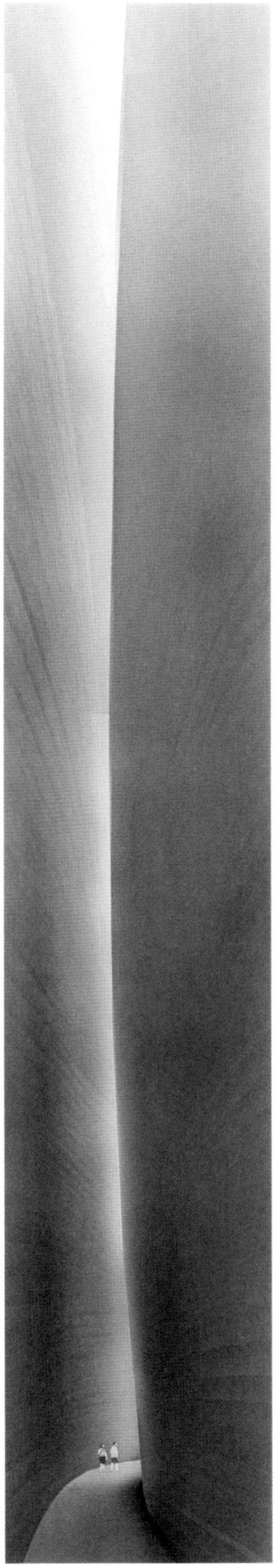

Eight villas, Dali

2016-

In these eight holiday homes in the mountains, adjacent to a riverbed, huge stone megaliths—characteristic of the region's landscape—form the basis of the project's concept, beginning with an investigation of the stones on the premises through a detailed site survey. Within the existing arrangement and location of these stones, opportunities were found for living spaces. The series of residences fit among the stone landscapes with only small adjustments, sometimes moving, removing, or adding them where needed. These megaliths not only create the houses' spatial composition, but also serve as pillars to support the large concrete roof, 300 m in length. The roof is done in an openwork style, allowing for large openings. Glass is fitted in and around the building so that what was formerly the exterior becomes the interior, creating a meandering landscape as a megalithic inside space. The lines of the building follow the hillside's descending slope. The edifice is divided into eight villas, each with an area of approximately 500 m², and occupying one of the eight stepped terraces.

Floor plan

Section

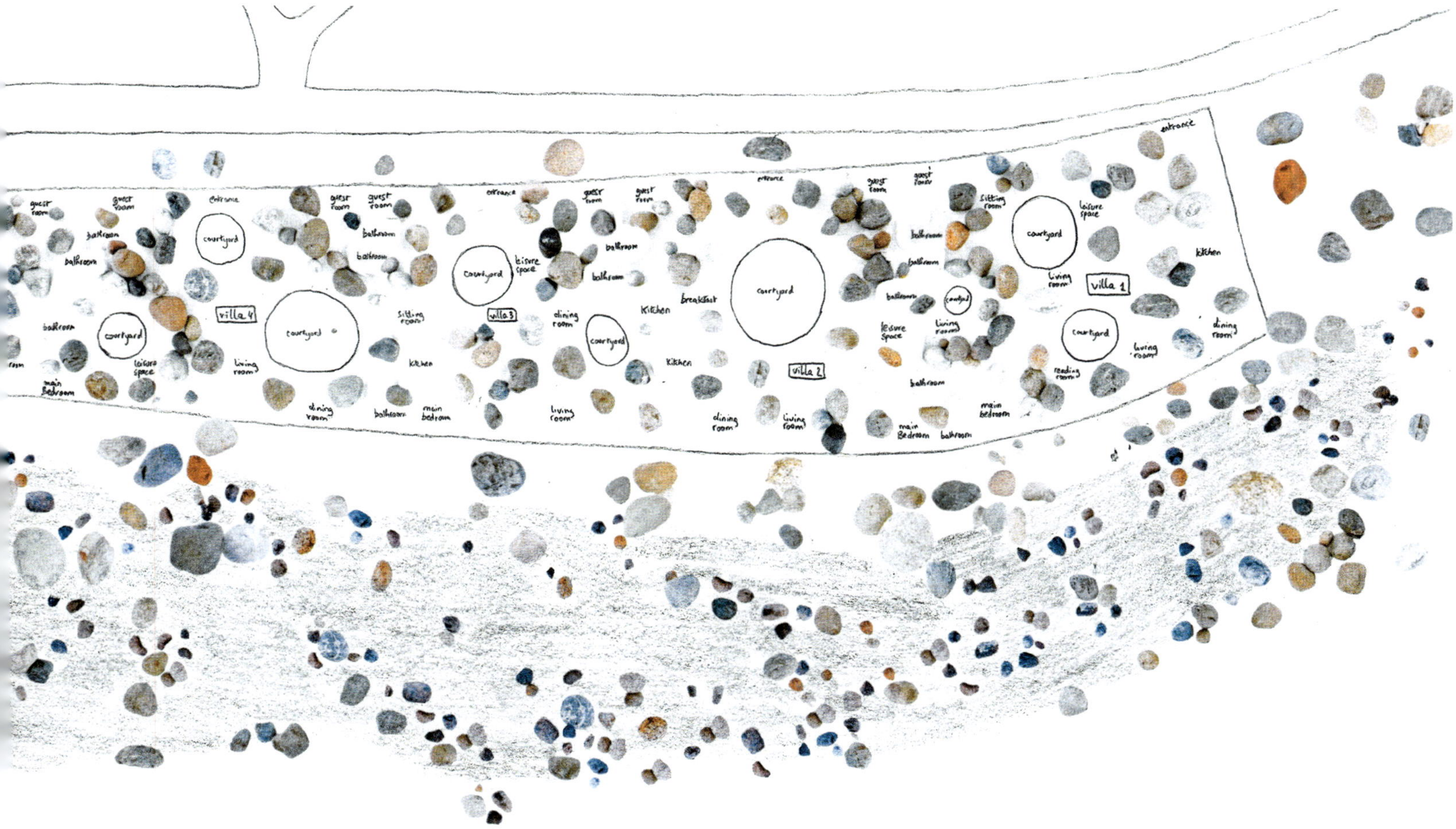
villa 1
villa 2
villa 3
villa 4
courtyard
entrance
kitchen
breakfast

0 5 20 m

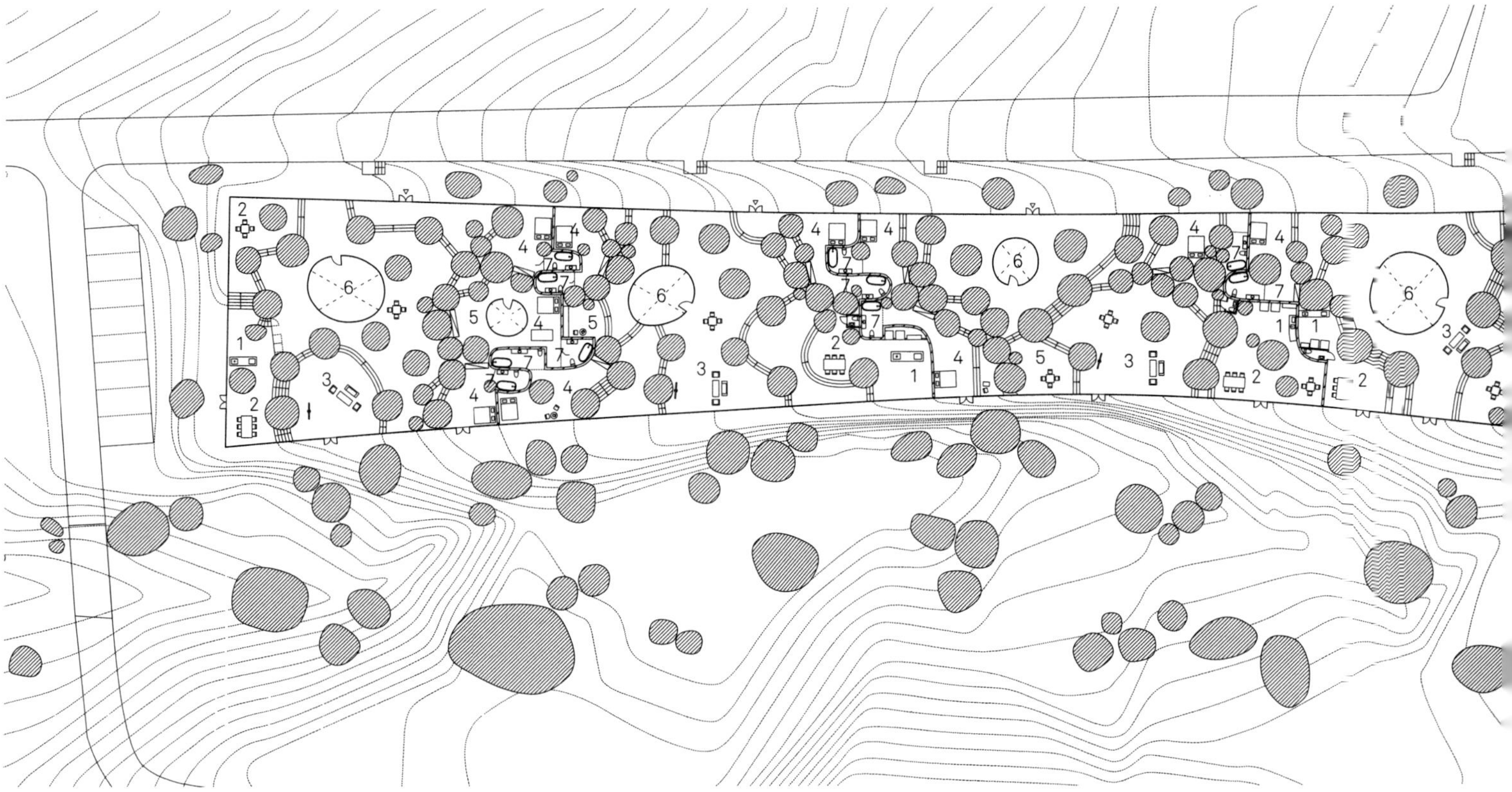

Floor plan

1 Kitchen
2 Dining room
3 Living room
4 Bedroom
5 Reading room
6 Courtyard
7 Bathroom

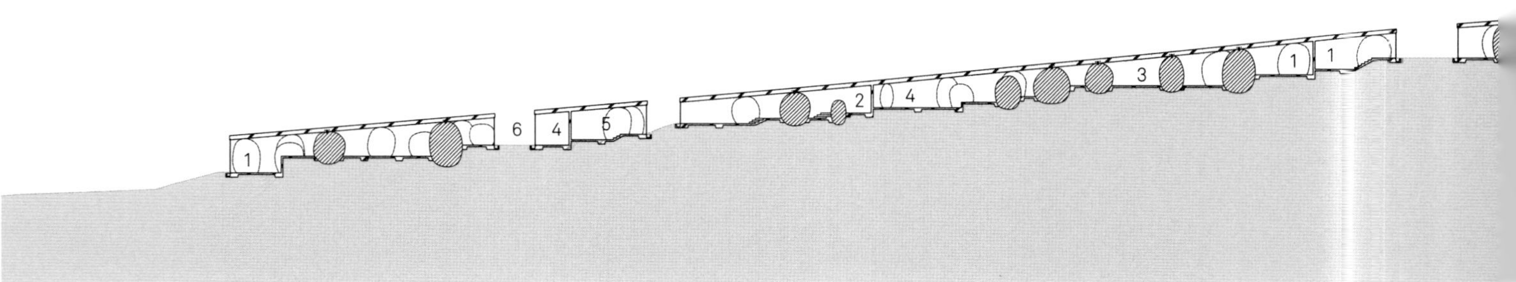

Section

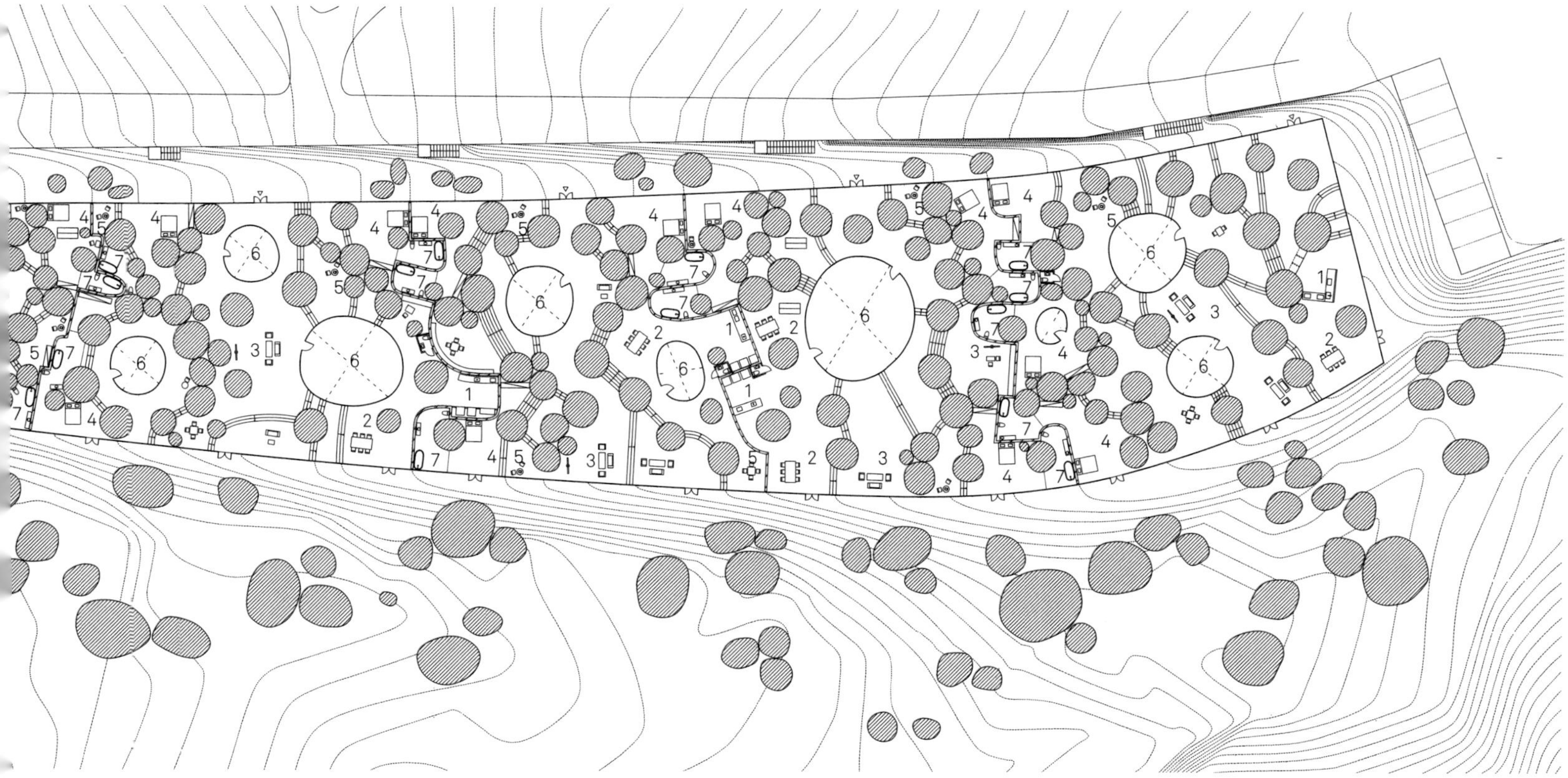

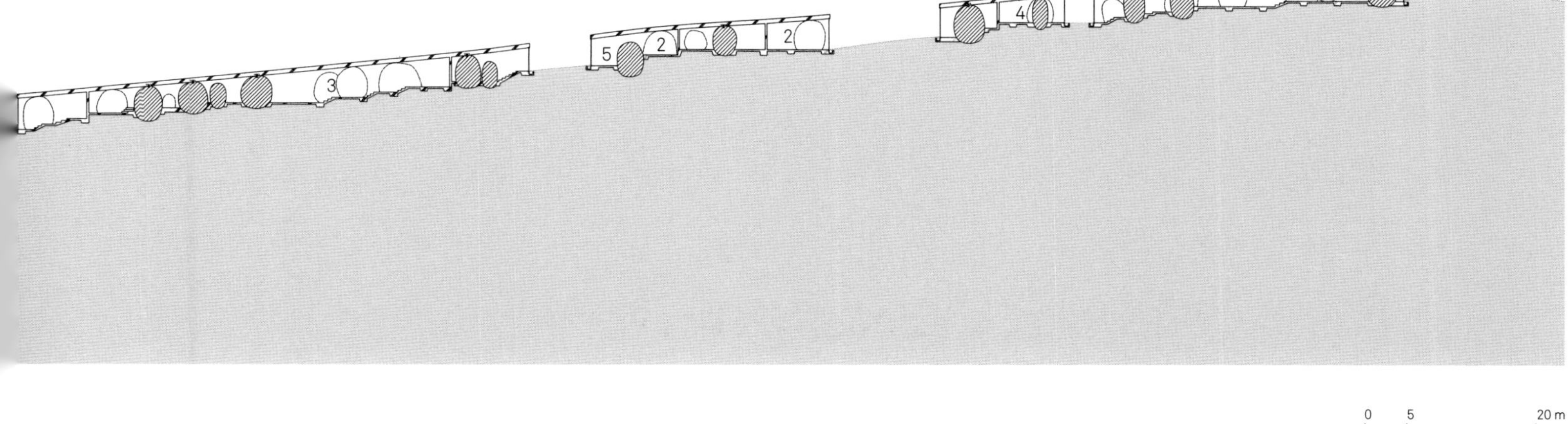
0 5 20 m

Cultural center, Shandong

2016-

Like a great walkway in the middle of the water, a narrow belt, albeit of variable width, crosses a lake from side to side in the Chinese wetlands of Bailuwan. The water penetrates under the glass partitions that serve as exterior walls. Visitors are invited to follow this covered path, bordered by two shores, which varies in width from 5 to 20 m. The entrance can be found at either end of the building, which visitors can traverse in full, discovering over the course of their stroll a variety of areas designed as a visitor center, relaxation and dining spaces, an exhibition area, and shops. The sinuosity of the building, the transparency of the lateral walls, and the continual presence of the water all lead to the creation of a new landscape, in which built and natural elements merge and become one.

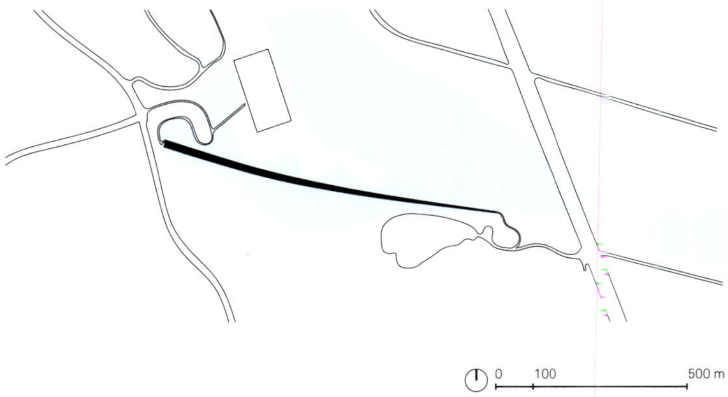

Floor plan

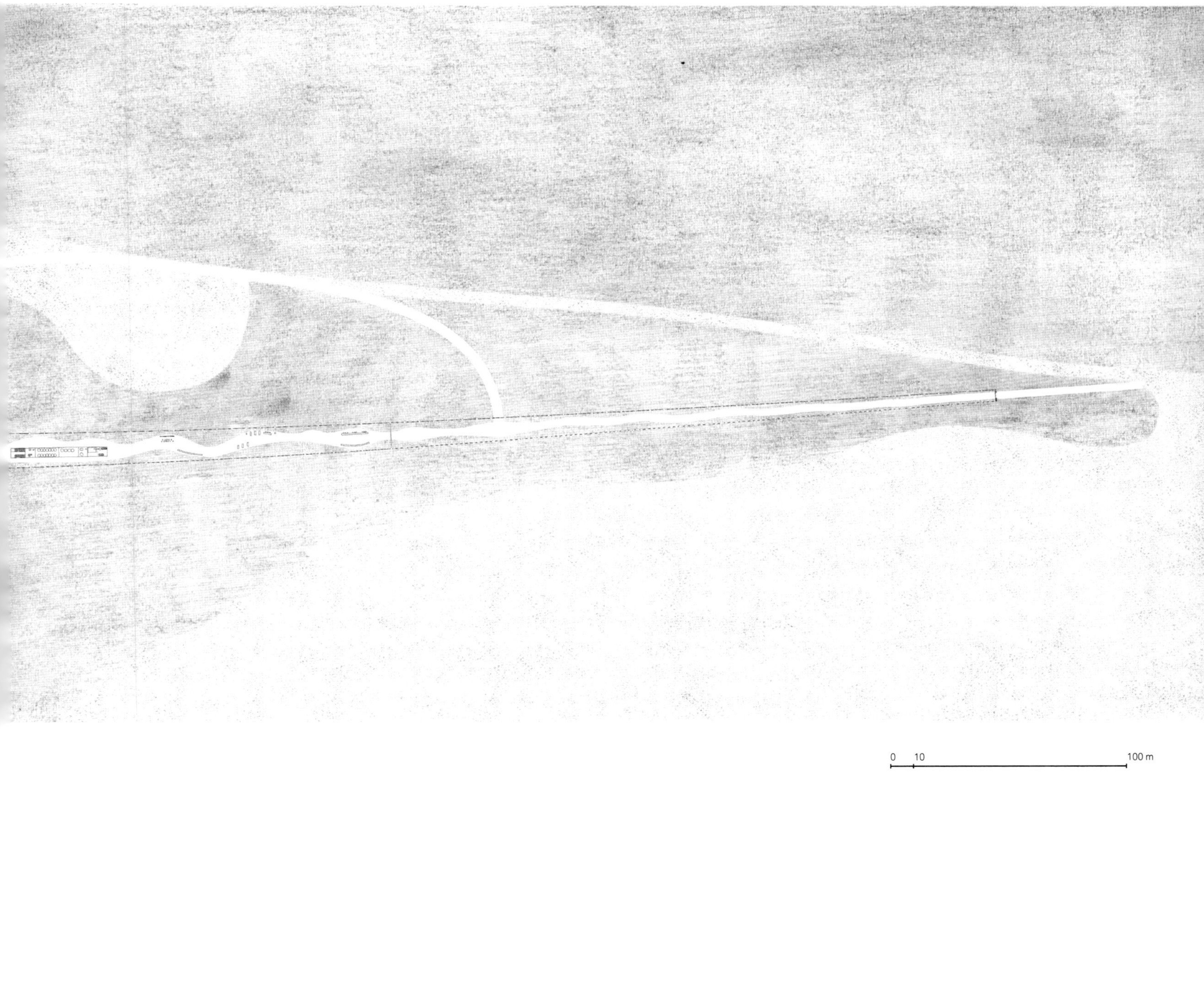
0
10
100 m

Cultural center, Shandong

JINS Eyewear Shop, Shanghai

2018

This store for a well-known Japanese brand of eyewear is situated in the shopping mall of the Shanghai World Financial Center in the city's Lujiazui financial district. The project's greatest challenge had to do with making a small shopping center store of some 140 m² architecturally significant amid the chaos of businesses and visitors. To that end five cantilevered display tables were built, fixed to one side of the shop, thereby freeing up the ground plane. Built of reinforced concrete, one of the tables has a cantilever of 12 m. The idea of taking the dimensions to the limit—maximum longitude without support and minimum width and depth—provides a display system for the eyewear and a to-and-fro circulation through the five display "fingers" situated at a height of 80 cm from the ground. When moving around the store the buyers can only be seen from the waist up, and from a floor-level view we see an entire horizontal landscape of legs between the floating tables, which seem to float by magic. The structure of the 25 cm deep tables is of prestressed steel covered by concrete in situ.

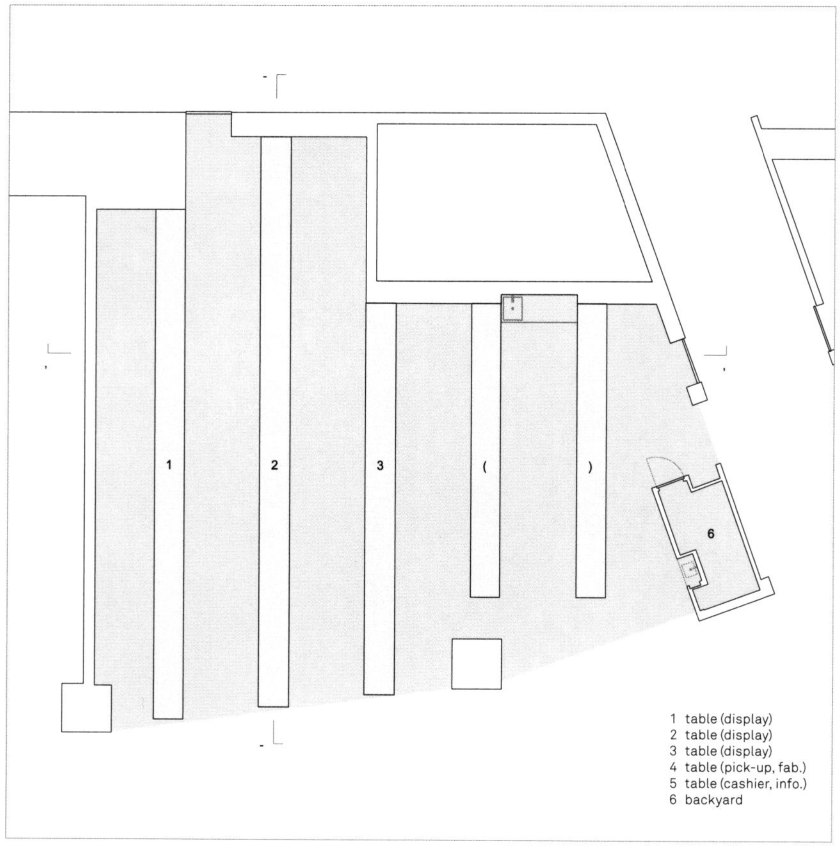

Floor plan

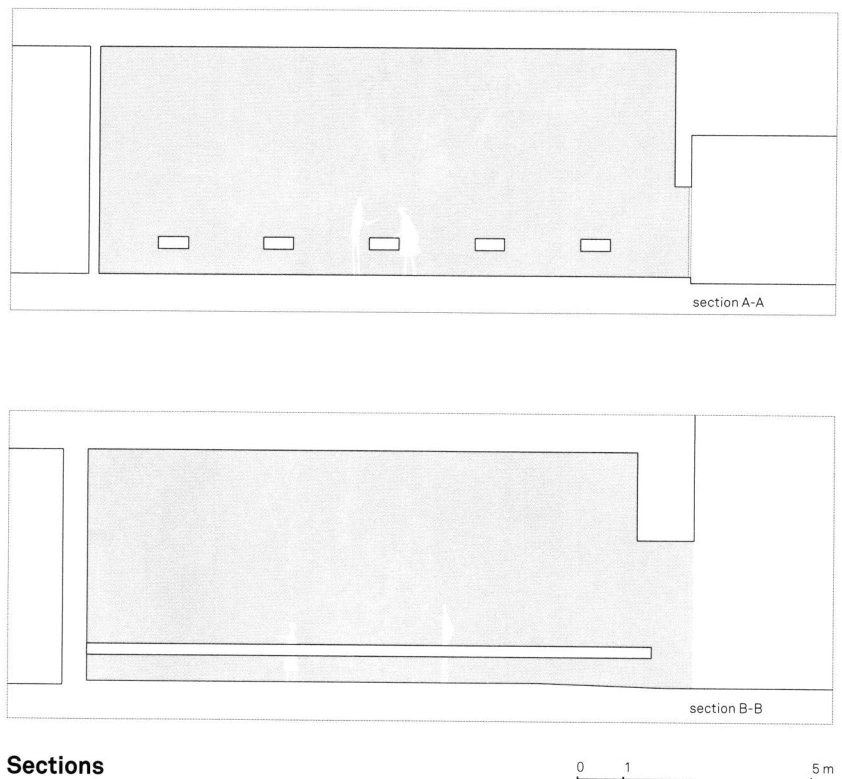

Sections

Credits

KAIT Workshop, Kanagawa

Location Kanagawa, Japan
Principal architect Junya Ishigami
Project team Harushi Chousa, Motosuke Mandai, Sachie Morita
Design and construction years 2004-2008
Structural engineers Konishi
Client Ikutoku Gakuen/Kanagawa Institute of Technology (KAIT)
Surface area 1,990 m^2
Photographs junya.ishigami+associates
Drawings Courtesy Collection Fondation Cartier pour l'art contemporain, Paris: pp. 12, 13

Yohji Yamamoto Store, New York

Location New York, USA
Principal architect Junya Ishigami
Project team Motosuke Mandai, Sachie Morita, Takahiko Sakue
Construction years 2006-2008
Local architects Ralph Sobel
Mechanical engineer Jack Stone
Photographs junya.ishigami+associates

Japanese Pavilion, Venice Architecture Biennale, Venice

Location Japanese Pavilion, Biennale Gardens, Venice, Italy
Principal architect Junya Ishigami
Project team Keisuke Fujiwara, Sachie Morita, Motosuke Mandai
Design and construction year 2008
Structural engineer Jun Sato
Botanist Hideaki Ohba
Photographs junya.ishigami+associates

Multipurpose plaza, Kanagawa

Location Kanagawa, Japan
Principal architect Junya Ishigami
Project team Taeko Abe, Motosuke Mandai, Sachie Morita, Kei Sato, Shuma Tei, Toru Yamada
Design and construction years 2008-
Client Ikutoku Gakuen/Kanagawa Institute of Technology
Structural engineer Jun Sato
Surface area 4,110 m^2
Photographs junya.ishigami+associates
Drawings Courtesy Collection Fondation Cartier pour l'art contemporain, Paris: pp. 38, 39, 44-45

House with plants

Location Japan
Principal architect Junya Ishigami
Project team Sachie Morita, Akira Uchimura
Design and construction years 2010-2012
Structural engineer Jun Sato
Surface area 100 m^2
Photographs junya.ishigami+associates
Drawings Courtesy Collection Fondation Cartier pour l'art contemporain, Paris: pp. 46, 48, 49

Polytechnic Museum, Moscow

Location Moscow, Russia
Principal architect Junya Ishigami
Project team Taeko Abe, Yuki Horikoshi, Soichi Inami, Alexandra Kovaleva, Kei Sato, Wataru Shinji, Kevin Walsh
Design and construction years 2012-
Client Polytechnic Museum Development Foundation
Surface area 39,870 m^2
Photographs Collection Fondation Cartier pour l'art contemporain, Paris

Park Groot Vijversburg Visitor Center, Tytsjerk

Location Tytsjerk, The Netherlands
Principal architect Junya Ishigami
Project team Taeko Abe, Terutaka Ide, Wataru Shinji, Shuma Tei, Akira Uchimura
Partner architect Studio Maks/Marieke Kums
Design and construction years 2012-2017
Client Park Vijversburg
Structural engineer Jun Sato
Surface area 245 m^2 (new construction), 350 m^2 (renovation)
Photographs Giovanni Emilio Galanello, Laurian Ghinitoiu, junya.ishigami+associates
Drawing Courtesy Collection Fondation Cartier pour l'art contemporain, Paris: p. 66

Home for the elderly, Akita

Location Akita, Japan
Principal architect Junya Ishigami
Project team Yuichi Uehara, Takashi Matsuda, Akihiro Yamaya
Design and construction years 2012-
Structural engineer Jun Sato
Surface area 560 m^2
Photographs junya.ishigami+associates
Drawings Courtesy Collection Fondation Cartier pour l'art contemporain, Paris: pp. 76, 77, 78-79, 80-81

Botanical Garden Art Biotop / Water Garden, Tochigi

Location Tochigi, Japan
Principal architect Junya Ishigami
Project team Taeko Abe, Gaku Inoue, Lucie Loosen, Akira Uchimura, Eiko Tomura,
Design and construction years 2013-2018
Client Yokozawa Farm Inc.
Structural engineer Jun Sato
Botanist Hideaki Ohba
Photographs nikissimo, junya.ishigami+associates,
Drawing Courtesy Collection Fondation Cartier pour l'art contemporain, Paris: p. 86

House and restaurant, Yamaguchi

Location Yamaguchi, Japan
Principal architect Junya Ishigami
Project team Taeko Abe, Atsushi Sato, Kei Sato
Design and construction years 2013-
Client Restaurant Noël
Structural engineer Jun Sato
Surface area 194 m^2
Photographs Yashiro photo office, Satoru Emoto, junya.ishigami+associates,
Drawings Courtesy Collection Fondation Cartier pour l'art contemporain, Paris: pp. 98, 100-101, 103, 104-105

Family house

Location Japan
Principal architect Junya Ishigami
Project team Taeko Abe, Masayuki Asami, Akira Uchimura
Design and construction years 2013-
Structural engineer Jun Sato
Surface area 128.5 m^2
Drawings Courtesy Collection Fondation Cartier pour l'art contemporain, Paris: pp. 106, 107, 108, 109, 110-111

Forest kindergarten, Shandong

Location Shandong, China
Principal architect Junya Ishigami
Project team Taeko Abe, Gagas Firas Si[illegible]ni, Alexandra Kovaleva, Zenan Li, Wataru Shinji, Akira Uchimura
Design and construction years 2015-
Client Shandong Rizhao Bailuwan Town
Structural engineer Jun Sato, CCDI Group
Surface area 5,400 m^2
Drawings Courtesy Collection Fondation Cartier pour l'art contemporain, Paris: pp.113, 114-115, 116-117

Chapel of the Valley, Shandong

Location Shandong, China
Principal architect Junya Ishigami
Project team Taeko Abe, Zenan Li, Cing Lu, Kei Sato, Akira Uchimura
Design and construction years 2016-
Client Shandong Rizhao Bailuwan Town
Structural engineer Jun Sato, CCDI Group
Surface area 132 m^2
Drawings Courtesy Collection Fondation Cartier pour l'art contemporain, Paris: pp. 119, 120, 121, 122, 123)

Eight villas, Dali

Location Dali, China
Principal architect Junya Ishigami
Project team Taeko Abe, Jaehyub Ko, Tong Zhang, Zenan Li
Design and construction years 2016-
Client Dali Yangbi Shimenguan Tourism Development
Structural engineer Jun Sato
Surface area 5,300 m^2
Drawings Courtesy Collection Fondation Cartier pour l'art contemporain, Paris: pp. 125, 126-127, 128-129, 130-131

Cultural center, Shandong

Location Shandong, China
Principal architect Junya Ishigami
Design team Zenan Li, Zhi Rui Lim, Rui [illegible]u, Tong Zhang, Sellua Di Ceglie
Partner architects CCDI Group
Design years 2016-
Client Shandong Rizhao Bailuwan Town
Structural engineers Jun Sato, CCDI Group
Surface area 3,000 m^2
Drawings Courtesy Collection Fondation Cartier pour l'art contemporain, Paris: p. 132

JINS Eyewear Shop, Shanghai

Location Shanghai World Financial Center (SWFC), Shanghai, China
Principal architect Junya Ishigami
Design team Cing Lu, Akira Uchimura
Design and construction year 2018
Client JINS Co. Ltd., Japan
Structural engineer Jun Sato
Surface area 140 m^2
Photographs Eiichi Kano

NEXUS

Conversation with Junya Ishigami

Hans Ulrich Obrist

I wanted to begin with the beginning, how architecture came to you or how you came to architecture?

Well, initially I didn't know what architecture was. I just wanted to create something. Architecture was a sort of random choice. And then when I was at university I learned a lot about architecture. I gradually learned what it was. So, it wasn't that I was intrigued by architecture from the outset. It was more the results that got me interested in architecture.

Could you tell us about the architects that influenced you at the beginning?

Yes, you could say Le Corbusier, Mies van der Rohe… I had that kind of hero in mind. They really opened up new, unknown horizons to me. And they are people who never cease to charm me.

Hans Ulrich Obrist (Zurich, 1968) is an art curator, critic and historian of art. He is artistic director at the Serpentine Galleries, London. Obrist is the author of The Interview Project, an extensive ongoing project of interviews. He is also co-editor of the revue *Cahiers d'Art*.

Conversation held on July 9, 2018 at the Fondation Cartier pour l'art contemporain in Paris on the occasion of the exhibition *Junya Ishigami, Freeing Architecture* (30 March - 9 September 2018).

What was the link with the Japanese avant-garde movement of the 1960s? I was very curious with regards to Metabolism because you mention it often to me. It's an extraordinary movement with Kisho Kurokawa, Kiyonori Kikutake, Fumihiko Maki and others... Many of these architects are now dead. Maki is still active. What was the influence this generation of Metabolist architects had on you?

I'm not sure the Metabolism movement had that much of a direct impact on me. But Metabolism as such has a very Japanese spirit. It is an actual system that was created and I don't think it is just Japan. There is a worldwide concept of the Metabolism movement, and I identify with it. There is Kenzo Tange for example. At the time he tried to make Japan uniform with concrete architecture. There was a lot of activity and that is something that intrigues me even now.

Have you been influenced by any other disciplines? Any inspiration other than architecture, such as art or other areas?

Yes, I like nature and gardens very much. So anything hinging on nature and gardens. And it's not just a pleasure for the senses. There's also a link with science and that is what attracts me. There is a Japanese scientist, Torahiko Terada, who was able to establish a link between literature and science. And this actually had an impact on me. It gives science an artistic sense and by creating the link with literature he's someone who interests me a lot.

I wanted to talk for a moment about Kazuyo Sejima, because it was truly unforgettable for me going into that firm in the early 2000s, into those offices where everything seemed to defy gravity. It was the opposite of gravity. Even the models appeared to swish in the breeze. There was an extraordinary atmosphere in those offices. Could you tell us more about these magical moments working there with Sejima and what inspiration it generated in you?

Yes, when I worked for Sejima, it was just after my four years at university, although I'd also worked there during my degree. As a student of Architecture I had a number of subjects I had to study and I was very frustrated by the subjects we are given in the School of Architecture. We didn't actually build anything. An aspect of reality was missing and I found it hard to get interested in this unrealistic material. Whereas in the firm everything we thought up could materialize. There was a sort of dynamism there, and even as a student it was very interesting. The whole process became clear. "Ah, okay, that's how it takes shape, how it becomes real." And at the time as a student I thought that they were on the same level, except they had that extra layer of reality. This afforded me a new experience and is what kept my enthusiasm for architecture alive.

And obviously, this layer of reality leads us directly to the exhibition *Freeing Architecture* (Fondation Cartier, Paris, 2018) because all this is reality. Often in exhibitions there are models, but of unbuilt designs. In this exhibition the models you show are either of designs that have been built or are in the process. But before we talk about them, and we will go through the exhibition and talk about its four areas, first I wanted to ask you to tell us, after working for Sejima, how did your career start? In any *catalogue raisonnée* there is always a No.1, a moment where the artist feels the work of the student is over. Where the body of work begins. What is your No.1? Tell us about your beginnings.

I left Sejima's firm in 2004 and I created a workshop at the Kanagawa Institute of Technology, where there were lots of pillars. I'd already been commissioned to produce this towards the end of my time with Sejima, so I think that this can be described as my first production.

Here in the exhibition we are in the built reality. But I was wondering whether you started with utopian projects or whether from the outset it was very concrete? Did you imagine utopian projects?

Yes, at the time when I had just started my own firm, most commissions were projects to be produced. But there were also projects that didn't have that aim. With regards to utopia, to me utopia is something that always comes with a measure of reality. When I was working at the firm none of our projects were completely imaginary. Everything, generally, was linked to a client. There were conditions and what we did was only provide suggestions in relation to the conditions that the client gave us.

In our first interview with Sejima, when she curated the Venice Biennale, in a very specific context, Sejima invited architects to produce pieces. Not just models, but to produce something in the space. And in the middle of that she created a space she designed with that "rabbit chair." They wanted me to interview each architect present at the exhibition to create a portrait of the Biennale. I found my notes and what I remember is that you talked to me about eliminating the

boundaries between nature and architecture. And this leads us directly to the first room, the first chapter of the exhibition at the Fondation Cartier. The first project we looked at together is this extraordinary Visitors Center in Park Vijversburg in The Netherlands. The visitors center follows a pathway, much like a promenade, inviting visitors to stroll. In a way the building follows a park. No trees were destroyed. So, in some ways the architecture was built respecting the trees. And here, in this magnificent garden, as Etel Adnan says, a day without trees isn't a day at all. So, I wondered whether you could tell me about this idea of eliminating the borders between architecture and nature, and particularly this first chapter of the exhibition on nature and environment that starts with this center in The Netherlands.

We talk about artificial architecture but I want my architectural works to blend into nature and become part of it. So for me there shouldn't be any boundary between architecture and nature. That is my default definition. So it's not a word that I try to remove. This boundary between architecture and nature… there simply shouldn't be a boundary between them, or at least that's my goal. And that is why in the first space I try to combine the natural space and architecture so that there is continuity. Architecture should be the continuation of the natural space. So that is why I show this as my first project.

There are also those other extraordinary designs in China, which is on a completely different scale, but also respects the same principal. These aren't megastructures but they are very big buildings, one horizontal, one vertical. One is a sort of chapel that is a valley in the valley and the other is a very big structure—one kilometer long—that is horizontal. Could you talk to us about these two designs?

Yes, the two designs in China. I could see the scale of the natural environment itself. In general architecture is based on a human scale. Indeed, architecture has always been designed around human beings. The human was at the center. Whereas in my case, I wanted to try and extend the limits of architecture while respecting this human scale. But I really wanted to ensure cohabitation between man and nature. And that is why in this design that is one km long in China, there was a lake and I wanted to keep the same scale. I wanted to preserve this impression that there could be a building, but that we were still walking around the lake. And as for the valley in China, it is a relatively narrow valley. I wanted the architecture to create a new environment in an environment that existed already. Thanks to these two designs we can see that architecture can further align with the natural scale. This is really a design that allows us to experiment with that scale.

So, turning to the chapel, which is the largest model in the first room, this valley in a valley is a very tall structure and it's also a vehicle for light, you told me earlier. Can you tell us more about it? Because what happens in this building with the light is quite extraordinary.

Yes, that's right, there is a chapel and I think that in all chapels in general light is a very important feature. And also the fact that the chapel could bring the light to the bottom of the valley made it a project that interested me a lot. Imagine that you are in a vast prairie. You get to see sunlight for a long time. Whereas if you're at the bottom of the valley, in a town or a small village, exposure to sunlight can be very short. This valley environment meant that there was a very different way of feeling the natural environment and I wanted to be in harmony with that and produce architecture that went hand in hand with that concept. The valley existed already and I wanted to go to even greater extremes with this concept, producing something that was even higher. I wanted to make the relationship between the valley and the sunlight into something even more spectacular, more spiritual.

And to conclude our discussion of this first space, there is that remarkable design we discussed at length earlier, a sort of cartography of trees, where you moved trees from one site to another. You cleared the site as the client, a restaurant, requested. You replanted them one-by-one in a second site, creating mini lakes all around them. It's like that first building you described. It's the trees that establish the shape of the structure. Could you talk to us about that?

Yes, this project was two designs in one. That is why there are two sites. On the first site there had to be a hotel, and on the second site we had to create a garden. For the site with the hotel, there was a forest there. For the garden, we had this idea of a prairie. For the hotel we had to get rid of the trees. So that is why I decided to move them to the new site to generate a new environment. Another factor was that this site was like a rice paddy, so there was a forest environment and a rice paddy environment and I wanted the two to overlap. I wanted to create a new natural environment. And in fact, what is natural is not that human beings play absolutely no part in it at all. I believe there are natural environments that exist thanks to human intervention. This is particularly the case in Japan. It happens often. In Japan in general it's rare to have completely natural environments. There are many natural environments in Japan that only exist thanks to human intervention. Consequently, rather than simply clearing out this forest I wanted to go inside it and move it elsewhere, thus creating a new natural environment.

In an earlier conversation you told me that architecture and the environment are continually changing and that you don't seek to use architecture to control them, but that you create an initial condition. You prepare what can be seen as a starting point and then it develops a life of its own. This is something that has always interested me about my medium, which is the medium of exhibitions, and about how one designs exhibitions. As curator you create the initial conditions but then the exhibition takes on a life of its own and continues to develop. So I was very interested to see how you relate that to architecture. How can one create something without controlling the starting point?

Well, it's hard to establish a starting point… but when architecture becomes natural it is a fascinating process, something completely new, something completely artificial. But gradually over time things change and this process can become part of architecture. If we take it to an extreme, then we have ruins which I think are somewhere between architecture and landscape. We can see how things evolve between something that is completely new and the ruin, and in between, the process of architecture that starts to merge into nature. As an architect I don't think this is something we can create or manage. It's more about how people will use this architecture. And so all we can do as architects is just create this starting point. But that is all we can do.

That also implies a certain change in the role of the architect, I suppose. Earlier, we discussed the fact that ten or twenty years ago there were these major themes in architecture, and one was the prototype. Do you think that it is less prominent these days and that the role of the architect has changed, has moved away from this idea of proposing prototypes. I was curious about this and wondered if you could talk to us about this new role for the architect and how you see the role of the architect in the twenty-first century.

Yes. As I said earlier, Le Corbusier and Mies van der Rohe are architects that I like a lot. There is a clear direction, a way of envisaging the future and a new way of living. One of these possible futures was many people looking exactly in the same direction and I think their vision came from that. But in the twenty-first century the scenario is no longer the same. Not everyone looks in the same direction. Everyone, individually, is looking at a different future and attempts to head towards this potential future. So as architects we don't have one single solution or response. There are all these people with their different futures in view. And I think that we have to offer architecture that is aligned with all these futures. So our new role is not to provide a single solution but rather to find a solution that adapts to all these futures and has plenty of possibilities.

Turning to the city, a few years ago I went to Rio to interview Oscar Niemeyer. I had been promised he spoke very good French and that an interpreter wouldn't be necessary. When I got there, he was aged 100 or 101 and he said, "Today I don't feel like speaking French. I'm going to speak Portuguese." There was a major problem because I did not understand what he said. He understood my questions but I didn't understand his answers. So, it was rather like an Exquisite Corpse game, as my next question had no link to his answer. And he also made it clear that he was 100 years old, he'd given thousands of interviews and did not really want to do any more. So I thought for a long time about how we could motivate Niemeyer to give an interview. I was with Norman Foster in Switzerland, in the mountains and the snow, and Foster was telling me he was building this ecological town in the desert, near Abu Dhabi. We were talking about this ecological town and Brasilia. I asked Norman if he had ever visited Brasilia, as I had just been to Brazil a few months earlier to meet Niemeyer. He told me he had never been to Brazil and had never met Niemeyer. I thought it was incredible that Foster and Niemeyer had never met. So, I spoke to him about bringing Foster to visit him. He was totally excited by the idea and this led to that long interview where we recorded the conversation between the two around this idea of inventing a city for the twenty-first century with the visions of Niemeyer and Foster. And I am very curious about this idea of something different, what you just described. Does that make it impossible to conceive a new city or town, or is it still possible, just by doing it differently?

Yes, the twentieth century was the era of the city. Architecture was there to envisage cities. In the twenty-first century we can't only think at the city scale. If we only focus on cities, we won't be able to resolve our current problems. These problems are on a planetary scale and we need to think on that scale. Urban space itself is shifting, and if we only think in terms of the city then our creativity and the innovations we can propose will be much too small. So there is a new environment where humans will work and have an effect on nature and that is how I think we can revise and revolutionize our lifestyles for the twenty-first century.

This brings us to the second room and the second chapter of the exhibition, where there is also a link with Niemeyer. Niemeyer was always drawing feverishly on huge sheets of paper. He would toss each one onto the floor until there were hundreds of sheets there. The last time I saw him, he no longer drew on paper, but he drew in the air and it was very beautiful. It was immaterial but he continued to

draw. We filmed it. It was quite magical. And this came back to me today when I saw the large model for Sydney because it's rather like a sketch in the air, don't you think? Like a sketch that can be seen differently from all angles. It's like a line drawn in the air. Could you talk to us about that, as it really is the dominant item? The model of the chapel dominated the first room, in the second room it's the model for Sydney, a design that is actually in the process of being completed in Australia. It would be lovely if you could tell us more about that.

Yes, for Sydney the brief was to make a new arch, a new gateway opposite Sydney City Hall. The arch was to be 60 meters high. The request was for an arch, a monument. Rather than put forward a shape I wanted to put forward something that could be appreciated in that same way, but visualized differently by each person. The vision I had was a cloud. Everyone experiences clouds in the same way, but no two clouds are alike. I wanted to create something that brought everyone together but that everyone conjured up differently. The idea was to create the impression that something had been sketched in the air, in space, like a cloud. Depending on where in the city you viewed the arch from, it would take on a completely different shape. Generally people are not all gathered in the same place. Each person would be able to visualize the monument completely differently. So it is one single monument but not a single shape. I wanted to create something with a different stature.

As you described it yourself, the design is like a sketch in the air. If we come back to the idea of sketching, doodling, when I last visited Umberto Eco in his house in Milan, he was very concerned that the art of handwriting was disappearing. He said that we were losing our ability to write with a pen, that calligraphy was disappearing. This led me to decide to post sketches and doodles and handwriting on my Instagram page every day and to use social media as a form of protest about this disappearance. During my last conversation with Zaha Hadid she also talked about that. She had always kept her remarkable drawings and her calligraphy, and we made an exhibition of them. She showed them to me. They were never in her studio, but rather at home, like a sort of treasure of her great imagination. She is often described not only as a pioneer of architecture but also of digital architecture. Everything in fact derives from these drawings, this calligraphy, these doodles. Now, I was intrigued because in the exhibition there are also these magnificent collages and sketches, and I'd like you to tell us something about the importance of drawing and doodling, because if I'm not mistaken you have a team that works with you on your models and your collages but you actually start with a sketch, don't you?

In my architecture all the sketching and doodling is going to be the basis for the final design. I use drawings to help me think through how I am going to develop the architecture. There are freehand sketches, slightly distorted handmade models, for example, and it is very interesting to see the effects of all this freehand work. Architecture in particular is something that goes from one scale to another. With models there is a real space. And in this limited space we sometimes find the space of the universe. Then we jump from scale to scale and that is how we broaden our thinking. So, these sketches are not just doodles for me, they actually represent a certain space. And how do we produce this space? This space that I just quickly sketched. It is very important for me to understand how it is going to materialize. And it is precisely because it was drawn freehand. How can this drawing be turned into architecture? That is my thought process.

And this first sketch brings me to childhood drawings, because you present two extraordinary kindergartens in this same room, not far from the drawing in the air for Sydney. Again, it is a question of scale. There are toys that suddenly become huge, enormous animals. Could you tell us something about that? I find these children's playground models truly magical.

As I said earlier, up until the twentieth century architecture placed humankind at its center. But now we have to see humankind as part of nature. So, the human scale must not be the only scale for architecture. We need to think of a new scale. And in terms of designs and the experimentation hinging on them, the question is what was the baseline scale? Generally there is a law governing architecture and it is based on this law that we produce architectural works. But all of that is based on the scale of the *adult* human being, the vision, the law, the scale, and the minimum height is based on the adult scale. But children have a completely different vision. To them a table could be seen to be a house. And we do not conceive architecture from a child's scale. In a kindergarten, for once, we can take a child's scale into account. Then we can think of things from an animal's scale or a plant's scale and that leads us to introduce a new type of scaling into architecture. That is also why I worked from the standpoint of children and animals. There was a children's playground and I tried to create a landscape for children. How do children see animals? I asked myself that question for this design. As adults we tend to observe landscapes from above. With this project I wanted to change that and for it to be us, the adults, looking upwards at a new landscape.

Then another dimension, which as you said earlier, consists of designs relating to the history of architecture. And I was also think-

ing that it was related to what Alison and Peter Smithson described as "as found," things we find as they are. In art we could even talk about the readymade, although I'm not sure we use this notion in architecture. Fredi Fischli showcased this in an exhibition at the Swiss Institute in New York. He described architecture as "ready-made." The idea undoubtedly is much more widely used in the art world. But this notion of "as found" is interesting, don't you think, because it is what is tied to designs at their very bottom. Firstly, there is this extraordinary design for this retirement home for patients with Alzheimer's, where you use a number of old Japanese homes from all over Japan which are ready-made and assembled and if I understand correctly, this approach helps these patients, by placing them in a familiar environment. Could you tell us more about this and how it evolved?

You just mentioned ready-made. For me, finding something that already exists and giving it new potential, that interests me a lot and intrigues me. Whenever you create a design you have to think about what existed already, whether man-made or natural, and for me, considering what already existed in this area is very important. Especially because there is an environment. We as architects cannot actually create something because time has had its impact. So how can we create a new space? This home for people with Alzheimer's was a sort of experiment. In Japan we tend to put Alzheimer's patients in a hospital. And in hospitals functionality is the most important feature. Space there has to be efficient. Above all it is designed to be efficient and have a very specific function. Of course I studied these spaces, and this functional architecture for these elderly people, I thought, was perhaps not such a familiar landscape for them. When you look at the sketches of Corbusier, for example, in general the architecture is designed for people in good health, providing sports facilities for example. So I realized that for people with disabilities or health problems the architectural landscape was less well adapted. I wondered how we could create something for people with disabilities or health problems, and that made me think of all the houses that existed already throughout Japan, and I wondered if we couldn't bring them all together and offer these people familiar surroundings. I thought this could be part of the solution. And in fact not all the houses are completely different. Many of the houses' modules are the same. The buildings are different but they can be assembled together. Even if they have been designed in completely different regions of Japan, the modules are essentially the same. So we can put them together in the same space. And as we are using old houses we generate the effect of time, which is something you can't do when building something totally new. Generally, in the garden even the stones… well it's not architecture that is going to create these stones. It just brought them together and put them in the garden. And for me here it was the same approach, bringing something that already existed and distributing it. That's what enables us to create a new space.

You just mentioned rocks. There are of course these houses, and here they are used as a ready-made entity, a sort of nature that will be destroyed in a few years. But in a certain sense you have framed the environment with these four villas as you found it and it seems to me to be a little like another ready-made example.

Yes, that's right. As I said earlier, creating something from something that already existed is very important to me. Take the design I mentioned at the beginning, the one in Holland. The garden was beautiful, it was protected by the government. It was an environment that no longer evolved. So how could I add an architectural element into this static environment? That was the design in The Netherlands. And when the natural environment no longer evolves architecture needs to find its place. On the other hand there is this design in China, in Dali, really not far at all from Tibet and very rocky. The region is renowned for that. It is a beautiful natural surrounding, and it shares that with the design for The Netherlands. But what is different is that in Holland the decision had already been taken that the natural environment could not be altered, as it was protected by the government. Whereas in China development had become widespread, and within two to three years this beautiful environment was going to be destroyed because of that development. What I wanted to do here was precisely the opposite of what I designed in Holland. It was to incorporate the existing environment into the architectural work.

Continuing in this vein, talking about as-found, there is a very big building in Moscow onto which you were asked to make an extension. A lot of buildings and museums build extensions. They add a new wing. But you did something much more unexpected here. You didn't create a new wing. Instead you started to dig. Can you tell us more about that?

Yes, here we're talking about the design in Moscow, an old polytechnic museum, and we had to renovate the building. Normally when you renovate an old building you add something such as a new roof or you renovate the façade, and generally renovations tend to stop there. Generally the historical committee will get involved in all the historical aspects. Here the historical committee wanted us to restore the building. But if we restored the façade it would give it a completely different image.

So, the historical committee wanted us to restore it to look roughly the same and it was very important that the building remained intact. That was the most important thing for the historical committee. I wanted to keep all the old features while at the same time breathe a little bit of modernity into them. How could I change this space yet maintain the same environment? So rather than adding something I tried to make the most of the underground space and expose it. This space had never been seen and revealing it gave the building a new scale. What had been the ground floor was no longer the ground floor, it was the first floor, and what had been the basement became the ground floor, meaning that the very proportions of the building were revolutionized. So I kept everything that was there and just offered some new architectural input for that project.

There is also the house that you designed for your parents, who have not yet retired. But as you said, this house is like a transition towards retirement. Once again something re-used, as it was your grandparents' house and has been remodeled for your parents. This leads me to a question. I wondered how you would draw a house for yourself? I'm always wondering what sort of house an architect would design for him or herself. I know you haven't designed it yet but I wonder whether you have any ideas. How would you imagine the house in which you yourself would live?

Well, in general when I design something my final decision about it is made on the due date. If I don't have a delivery date there are no definitive responses, so I would be constantly changing my ideas. Therefore if I had to design my own house there would be no delivery date and so I have the impression I would be eternally changing the design without being able to make up my mind.

So it could be an unfinished house?

In a sense, yes. The only condition that makes me complete an architectural work is the delivery date, so yes, you could look at it like that.

We have spoken a lot about your built designs, because the exhibition at the Fondation Cartier is focused on designs that have been or are being built. But of course an architect always has unbuilt designs. In all my interviews I always ask about projects that haven't been built. We know very little about the unproduced works of artists, writers, poets or composers. But we know a little more about those of archi-

tects as sometimes they publish them. Their range or scope is pretty vast and could include designs that are too big to be built, or too utopian, which brings me back to the issue at the beginning. Then there are some that are too small. At one time Cildo Meireles wanted to exhibit a one cubic meter cube in a museum, an otherwise completely empty museum. This was a project that could not be completed and it took her a long time to find a museum prepared to let her do it. So designs can be too big or too small. And then there are designs for competitions that were lost. This tends to be the main source of architects' non-developed work, rather like artists with public commissions. There are also designs that are politically censored. And as our friend Doris Lessing says, we must not forget those that we have not dared to do, because there may well be a form of auto-censorship with designs we don't dare take forward. So, there is a whole range of non-produced designs. Although I know it is not the purpose of this exhibition, I wondered if you could tell us about one or two of your favorite designs that are so far still on the drawing board but that you hope to produce in the future.

Yes, it's true that this exhibition is indeed based on what has been built. But if we talk about things that haven't been built, since 2004 there are designs that have not been completed, for instance when I haven't won a competition. And there are plenty of those. But if I had to select one, then it's quite difficult, especially as there are lots of designs that I have quite simply forgotten. So this is a difficult question. But if I have to choose one, it wasn't for a competition. A few years ago I did an exhibition that wasn't about presenting my built works but rather how I studied architecture. I showcased some of the designs I had conceived. Some had no clients. Others were impossible to build. Earlier we talked about China and that one kilometer long building. That was a design where I used the same scale as nature. But of all the types of designs that go beyond the scale of a city and blend into nature, some could not be built. If one day I could build these projects it would be very exciting for me. And if that happened we would see how with the modern means at our disposal we could attempt to make these designs materialize. That would interest me.

And the poet Rainer Maria Rilke wrote a magnificent book offering advice to a young poet. Given that there are lots of young architects in the audience, I was curious about what your advice would be for a young architect in 2018?

I started architecture and I have always had new and different projects. And sometimes my previous experience doesn't serve me in my new endeavors. So consequently I myself often feel like a young architect. That is why I wouldn't wish to give advice to other young architects. But what motivates me with architecture, and I'm happy to share that, is the landscape I see. That's what I build and that is my motivation as an architect. It's rather like when we want to travel. There is a landscape out there that we don't know and when we travel we discover that landscape. Architecture is the same: there is a landscape we want to see and we will create it. That is my main motivation as an architect and if that can serve as a clue for young architects then it is what I would like.

Biography

Junya Ishigami

Junya Ishigami (Kanakawa Prefecture, Japan, 1974) studied Architecture at Tokyo University of the Arts. He began his career working at SANAA studio (2000-2004) before founding his own studio, junya.ishigami+associates, in Tokyo in 2004. He has been a visiting professor at Tokyo University of Science, Tohoku University, Harvard University Graduate School of Design, and Princeton University School of Architecture. He has published several books: *Plants + Architecture* (2010), *Another Scale of Architecture* (2011), *Small Images* (2103), *How Small? How Vast? How Architecture Grows* (2014), *Another Nature* (2015), and *Freeing Architecture* (2018).